FYI
FOR PERFORMANCE MANAGEMENT™

UNIVERSAL DIMENSIONS FOR SUCCESS

ROBERT W. EICHINGER
KIM E. RUYLE
MICHAEL M. LOMBARDO

TABLE OF CONTENTS

THE 10 UNIVERSAL PERFORMANCE DIMENSIONS

APPENDICES

INTRODUCTION

Performance counts. Execution. Accomplishments. Results. All the things organizations, managers, and employees are held accountable for. That's what performance is about.

The best managers of performance have a firm hand and a soft glove. They help their employees set stretch goals and then drive hard for results. They apply managerial courage by delivering timely, direct, honest, and actionable feedback. The best managers temper their results orientation by concern for their employees. They create a positive work environment. They coach and develop people. They build high-performing teams.

Performance management is a fundamental process owned and applied by bosses. Done well, performance management improves business results, increases employee engagement, and shapes and enhances the culture of the organization.

The process starts with aligned goal setting. Business objectives aligned with your organization's strategic intent start from the top and cascade down through each level all the way to individual contributors—so that everyone has meaningful stretch goals aligned with the strategy. The goals form the basis for an ongoing dialogue between bosses and employees and an opportunity for feedback and coaching. At the end of the business cycle, performance is reviewed and assessed against achievement of goals, against execution of the plan. The level of achievement, the measure of execution, should then be rewarded.

This book is about methods and tools that will improve the effectiveness of the performance management process. *FYI for Performance Management*™ is part of the PERFORMANCE MANAGEMENT ARCHITECT®, a suite of tools designed to improve *what* people accomplish and *how* they get the job done.

THE PERFORMANCE MANAGEMENT ARCHITECT® (PMA) SUITE INCLUDES:

- **The 10 Universal Performance Dimensions**
  The 10 Performance Dimensions are part of the Lominger LEADERSHIP ARCHITECT® Competency Library. Each Dimension represents a key aspect of how performance is achieved and has a corresponding ten-point behaviorally anchored rating scale (BARS). The Dimensions and BARS, in addition to being listed in this book in Appendix G, are available in a card deck format, the PMA Sort Cards, to facilitate training or group processes. The *PMA Quick Reference Guide* provides guidelines for using the PMA Sort Cards.

I

- **The PMA Placemat Set**
  The three placemats illustrate the application of the 10 Universal Performance Dimensions in the primary performance management phases—planning and goal setting, feedback and coaching, and performance review.

- This book, **FYI for Performance Management™**
  FYI for Performance Management™ is a comprehensive guide to applying the Dimensions for performance improvement. Included in the back jacket is the FYI for Performance Management™ Companion CD which is an added reference and training tool for incorporating the 10 Universal Performance Dimensions into a performance management process.

WHY IS PERFORMANCE MANAGEMENT IMPORTANT?

Performance management is not an annual event. It is not a project or an initiative. Performance management is a continuous process. Although there are typically milestone events and deadlines in a performance management cycle, the process should not be event-driven; it should be results-driven. The results are achieved in the three phases of the process: (1) planning and goal setting; (2) feedback and coaching; and (3) performance review and appraisal. The focus of these phases is, respectively, the beginning, middle, and end of the performance management cycle (typically corresponding to a business cycle, e.g., a fiscal year). However, these phases should not be regarded as having rigid starting or ending points. The ultimate objective is improved and sustained job performance.

Performance management includes planning, setting objectives, organizing work, communicating information, motivating employees, and managing consequences. These are the issues addressed by the process of performance management. Managers who effectively execute performance management are performing a significant portion of their management responsibility. Managers who don't execute performance management well (or don't do it at all) are negligent in a large part of their job.

As performance management is effectively executed, you can look for these significant impacts:

- **Business results improving.** Performance management aligns the goals and behaviors of individual employees with the business objectives of the organization. It gets team members pulling together to achieve shared objectives. It puts focus on things that matter—strategies, tactics, and capabilities that result in success as defined by the goals of the business.

- **Employees becoming more engaged.** Motivation increases when roles are better defined, performance expectations are clearer, the amount and quality of feedback increases, and there is a clear link between performance and rewards.

- **Culture of the organization growing stronger.** Performance management shapes the culture of the organization through the tone and execution of the process. The ongoing conversations between managers and employees establish expectations and provide a mechanism for explaining and demonstrating organizational values.

So, when done well, performance management has very meaningful benefits. A poorly executed performance management process can cause damage. Positive results don't come easily and are only achieved when individual managers take ownership and drive the process.

WHY ARE THE 10 UNIVERSAL PERFORMANCE DIMENSIONS IMPORTANT?

Performance goals describe *what* is to be achieved by the employee—the results. The 10 Universal Performance Dimensions indicate *how* the results are achieved.

Managers can identify all or some combination of the Dimensions to be applied against any goal:

- **Guide employees in doing their work.** Linking Dimensions to the goal puts focus on important behaviors and outcomes—quality, timeliness, productivity, cooperation, work habits, etc.

- **Facilitate feedback and coaching.** The behaviorally anchored rating scales (BARS) associated with the Dimensions provide very specific statements that can communicate how work is being done and how it should be done. It's easier for managers and coaches to help the employee "move the needle" on performance by using these statements when giving feedback and coaching.

- **Improve the review process.** When Dimensions are linked to performance goals, the BARS greatly improve the objectivity of evaluations and make review conversations more constructive and evaluation of performance more comfortably accepted by employees.

- **Lead employees to meaningful improvement opportunities.** The Dimensions are mapped to the Lominger Competency Library, and improvement in targeted competencies is the focus of development. Performance goals are about the what. The Dimensions are about the how. And competencies are about the how and why. In other words, if you want performance improvement in terms of work accomplishments (the what), work on improvements in the 10 Universal Performance Dimensions (the how). To do that, focus on improvements in the associated competencies.

III

WHO IS THIS BOOK FOR?

FYI for Performance Management™ is for three primary audiences:

- **Managers.** This book provides guidance for three of the tasks managers must perform: (a) communicating clear expectations, (b) providing feedback and coaching, and (c) reviewing and appraising performance. The 10 Universal Performance Dimensions and BARS will be used when collaborating with employees to set goals at the beginning of a performance management cycle. The BARS are very useful when incorporated into ongoing feedback and coaching and are used again during performance review. Of course, just as the remedies can be used for self-directed development and improvement, they can be used by managers when coaching employees and helping them prepare improvement plans. Each of these three management duties is further addressed in Appendices C, D, and E, and supported by the *FYI for Performance Management*™ *Companion CD*.

- **Coaches.** Anyone engaged in coaching for performance—internal coaches, mentors, managers, and external coaches—will find this book a helpful reference and tool to use for coaching. The Skilled and Unskilled descriptions are especially useful to provide awareness and establish a need for improvement. The remedies comprise ready-made elements for action plans. Appendix D specifically addresses how the 10 Universal Performance Dimensions can be used in a coaching situation.

- **Employees.** This book has improvement tips that will benefit people at any position level who are aware of improvement needs and are motivated to improve their job performance. The remedies provided can be used to create a self-directed improvement plan. Appendix A has a wealth of information on strategies for improvement, and Appendix B is a reproducible template for recording an improvement plan and for tracking progress. Appendix C has information to help you set meaningful performance goals.

WHERE DID THE PERFORMANCE MANAGEMENT ARCHITECT® COME FROM?

The 10 PERFORMANCE MANAGEMENT ARCHITECT® Dimensions were derived from studies on performance measurement. They apply to a wide variety of positions, from entry level to the boardroom. The Dimensions are part of the LEADERSHIP ARCHITECT® Competency Library which also includes the 67 Leadership Competencies, 19 Career Stallers and Stoppers, and 7 International Focus Areas. We have numbered the Dimensions from 81–90, fitting them in between the 1–67 Leadership Competencies (with space for more at some future time) and the 101–119 Career Stallers and Stoppers.

IV

Ten or more improvement remedies are provided for each Dimension. We developed these remedies after review of research studies related to competency development. In addition to the research, we have incorporated what we've learned from years of experience in the development business as researchers and practitioners. In our careers, we have coached thousands of executives and managers. We've heard them describe their difficulties, helped them figure out what's getting in their way, and tested our remedies with them. We know from experience and research what remedies and improvement tips are most likely to work.

In developing these remedies, our objectives were to achieve:

1. Brevity. We suspect you're busy and want to get started right away by going after the low-hanging fruit. The improvement tips are concise and enable you to start immediately and see results quickly.

2. Simplicity. We could have included numerous and complex improvement strategies. Instead, we limited the number of remedies for each Dimension and kept most of them simple because we believe they are more likely to lead people to take action, to actually do something to improve. For those interested in more lengthy treatments, we've recommended books as well.

3. Practicality. While some of our suggestions are involved and require long-term effort, most are practical things you can implement today to achieve some quick improvement.

HOW IS THIS BOOK ORGANIZED?

The ten chapters in *FYI for Performance Management*™ correspond to the 10 Universal Performance Dimensions, and each includes the following sections:

*   **Quotes**—To stimulate thinking about the particular Dimension.

*   **General Definition**—The Dimension defined.

*   **Unskilled**—Descriptors that apply to people who typically perform poorly in the Dimension. Associated leadership competencies are provided in this section that can serve to some extent as substitutes (skills that substitute a strength to attack a weakness) for the Dimension.

*   **Average**—Descriptors that apply to how people typically perform in the Dimension.

*   **Skilled**—Descriptors that apply to people who demonstrate exceptional strength in the Dimension.

*   **Overused Skill**—Descriptors that apply to people who overdo this Dimension and, in doing so, turn it from an asset into a liability. Associated leadership competencies are provided in this section that can serve to some extent as

V

compensators (skills that decrease the negative effect of strengths that have gone into overdrive) for the Dimension.

- **Some Causes**—Variety of root causes that can explain why people might do poorly in the Dimension.

- **The Map**—Reasons the particular Dimension is important.

- **Some Remedies**—Suggestions for actions to strengthen performance in this Dimension.

- **Suggested Readings**—Reference list of resources we've found useful in performance improvement in each Dimension. We've tried to identify books that are practical, useful, well written, and readily accessible.

Seven appendices provide support material to enable you to implement the 10 Universal Performance Dimensions in your performance management process.

- **Appendix A: Job Improvement Strategies**—General guidelines and strategies for improvement in any Dimension.

- **Appendix B: My Personal Improvement Plan**—Reproducible forms to help you plan and track improvement in selected Dimensions.

- **Appendix C: Planning and Goal Setting**—Guidelines for development of effective goals and methods of incorporating the Dimensions in goal setting. A goal-setting scenario illustrates additional information provided in the *FYI for Performance Management*™ *Companion CD*.

- **Appendix D: Feedback and Coaching**—Methods for using the Dimensions to improve the effectiveness of feedback and coaching sessions. A feedback and coaching scenario references the additional support from the *FYI for Performance Management*™ *Companion CD*.

- **Appendix E: Performance Reviews**—Suggestions for using the Dimensions to accurately review and appraise employee performance. A performance review scenario details further information referenced in the *FYI for Performance Management*™ *Companion CD*.

- **Appendix F: Mapping of the 10 Universal Performance Dimensions to the 67 Leadership Competencies and Associated Remedies**—A guide showing how the Dimensions, leadership competencies, and remedies are related.

- **Appendix G: Behaviorally Anchored Rating Scales (BARS) for Performance Management**—Very specific performance standards that communicate how work is being done and how it should be done.

- **Suggested Readings for Performance Management**—Additional resources for performance management in each Dimension.

The suggestions and resources provided in this book will enable individuals to improve their performance, coaches to be more effective, and managers to implement a performance management process that drives a high-performance culture in the organization.

Robert W. Eichinger
Kim E. Ruyle
Michael M. Lombardo

ABOUT THE AUTHORS

BOB EICHINGER

Bob Eichinger is CEO of Lominger International, A Korn/ Ferry Company and cofounder of Lominger Limited. He is cocreator of The LEADERSHIP ARCHITECT® Suite of management, executive, and organizational development tools. During his 40+ year career, he has worked inside PepsiCo and Pillsbury, and as a consultant in Fortune 500 companies in the U.S., Europe, Japan, Canada, and Australia. Bob lectures extensively on the topic of executive and management development and has served on the Board of the Human Resource Planning Society. He has worked as a coach with more than 1,000 managers and executives. Bob's books include *The Leadership Machine,* written with Mike Lombardo, and *100 Things You Need to Know: Best People Practices for Managers & HR,* written with Mike Lombardo and Dave Ulrich.

KIM RUYLE

Kim Ruyle is vice president of product for Lominger International. He started his career in the skilled trades, taught at several universities, founded and managed a software company, and held management positions in Fortune 500 and Global 100 organizations. In the human resource and learning and development fields, Kim has presented at national and international conferences, authored over a dozen book chapters and articles, and served on numerous expert panels. Kim coauthored *FYI for Strategic Effectiveness* with Bob Eichinger and Dave Ulrich.

MIKE LOMBARDO

Mike Lombardo has over 30 years experience in executive and management research and in executive coaching. He is also a cofounder of Lominger Limited and cocreator of The LEADERSHIP ARCHITECT® Suite of tools. With Bob Eichinger, Mike has authored 40 products for the suite, including *The Leadership Machine*, the *CAREER ARCHITECT®, CHOICES ARCHITECT®,* and *VOICES®.* During his 15 years at the Center for Creative Leadership, Mike was a coauthor of the *Lessons of Experience,* which detailed which learnings from experience can teach the competencies needed to be successful. He also coauthored research on executive derailment revealing how personal flaws and overdone strengths caused otherwise effective executives to get into career trouble. Mike has won four national awards for research on managerial and executive development.

ACKNOWLEDGEMENTS

We appreciate the assistance of all those who contributed expertise and assistance in the preparation of this book.

Lisa-Marie Hanson, George Hallenbeck, Ken De Meuse, and Paul Stiles, all from the terrific research and product development team at Lominger International, reviewed our work and made many helpful suggestions.

Diane Hoffmann, Lesley Kurke, and Eric Ekstrand, also on the product team at Lominger International, accommodated impossible deadlines and, once again, did a great job of reviewing and preparing the manuscript for production.

Several Lominger Associates reviewed materials and contributed useful ideas. Special thanks to Linda Hodge, Linda Rodman, Jane Schenck, Steve Marshall, Kathy Spinelli, Dan Moss, Kate Kessenich Bett, and Nicole Lambrou.

Bonnie Parks, as always, was wonderful to work with and did a superb job of reviewing and editing our manuscript.

QUANTITY OF OUTPUT OF WORK

Hard work spotlights the character of people: Some turn up their sleeves, some turn up their noses, and some don't turn up at all.
— Sam Ewing

General Definition: Quantity or amount of work produced personally or from a group or team on assignments/tasks/projects/products/or services without regard to any other factors like quality or timeliness of the work.

UNSKILLED

- ❏ Low amount of work produced
- ❏ Lags behind most other people or groups
- ❏ Significant goals are missed
- ❏ Productivity is lower than most others
- ❏ Makes a few goals but misses others

  Select one to three of the competencies listed below to use as a substitute for this Performance Management Dimension if you decide not to work on it directly.

  SUBSTITUTES: 1,14,15,16,18,19,20,24,25,36,39,43,52,59,61,63

AVERAGE

- ❏ Amount of work produced is acceptable and about like most other people or similar groups
- ❏ Most production goals are met; a few may be missed
- ❏ Work output is at standard

SKILLED

- ❏ The amount of work produced by this person or group is simply amazing
- ❏ No matter how high the production or output goals are set, more is produced than expected in all areas
- ❏ Almost always number one in productivity
- ❏ Defines hard work for the rest

OVERUSED SKILL

- ❏ The amount of work coming from this person or group is so high that sometimes quality and morale suffer because things are so intense and the pace is so fast
- ❏ Can be so single-mindedly focused on getting the most work out that all other matters including concern for others suffer

1

Select one to three of the competencies listed below to work on to compensate for an overuse of this skill.

COMPENSATORS: 7,17,20,23,33,36,41,42,50,52,60

SOME CAUSES

- ❏ Burned out
- ❏ Fights bosses
- ❏ Goals set too high
- ❏ Lack of ambition
- ❏ Lack of realistic resources
- ❏ New to the job or field
- ❏ Not aligned or committed
- ❏ Not focused or disciplined
- ❏ Not organized
- ❏ Organization politics
- ❏ Perfectionist
- ❏ Procrastinator

THE MAP

There is probably no substitute for getting things done. Most rewards in life go to those who produce. Being able to consistently produce covers a lot of other problems. Others are not very tolerant of excuses from those who consistently don't get things done. Once not getting things done surfaces as an issue, others begin to look for the reasons and begin finding other problems—real and imagined. It's a career death spiral. The best course of action is to concentrate fully on reaching the goals and objectives set for the task, project or job you are in or get out.

SOME REMEDIES

- ❏ **1. Setting priorities?** What's mission-critical? What are the three to five things that most need to get done to achieve your goals? Effective performers typically spend about half their time on a few mission-critical priorities. Don't get diverted by trivia and things you like doing but that aren't tied to the bottom line. *More help? – See #50 Priority Setting.*

- ❏ **2. Set goals for yourself and others.** Most people work better if they have a set of goals and objectives to achieve and a standard everyone agrees to measure accomplishments against. Most people like stretch goals. They like them even better if they have had a hand in setting them. Set checkpoints along the way to be able to measure progress. Give yourself and others as much feedback as you can. *More help? – See #35 Managing and Measuring Work.*

❑ **3. How to get things done.** Some don't know the best way to produce results. There is a well-established set of best practices for producing results—TQM, ISO and Six Sigma. If you are not disciplined in how to design work flows and processes for yourself and others, buy one book on each of these topics. Go to one workshop on efficient and effective work design. Ask those responsible for total work systems in your organization for help. *More help? – See #52 Process Management and #63 Total Work Systems (e.g., TQM/ISO/Six Sigma).*

❑ **4. Organizing?** Are you always short on resources? Always pulling things together on a shoe string? Getting results means getting and using resources. People. Money. Materials. Support. Time. Many times it involves getting resources you don't control. You have to beg, borrow, but hopefully not steal. That means negotiating, bargaining, trading, cajoling, and influencing. What's the business case for the resources you need? What do you have to trade? How can you make it a win for everyone? *More help? – See #37 Negotiating and #39 Organizing.*

❑ **5. Getting work done through others?** Some people are not good managers of others. They can produce results by themselves but do less well when the results have to come from the team. Are you having trouble getting your team to work with you to get the results you need? You have the resources and the people but things just don't run well. Maybe you do too much work yourself. You don't delegate or empower. You don't communicate well. You don't motivate well. You don't plan well. You don't set priorities and goals well. If you are a struggling manager or a first-time manager, there are well-known and documented principles and practices of good managing. Do you share credit? Do you paint a clear picture of why this is important? Is their work challenging? Do you inspire or just hand out work? Read *Becoming a Manager* by Linda A. Hill. Go to one course on management. *More help? – See #18 Delegation, #20 Directing Others, #36 Motivating Others, and #60 Building Effective Teams.*

❑ **6. Working across borders and boundaries?** Do you have trouble when you have to go outside your unit to reach your goals and objectives? This means that influence skills, understanding, and trading are the currencies to use. Don't just ask for things; find some common ground where you can provide help. What do the peers you're contacting need? Are your results important to them? How does what you're working on affect their results? If it affects them negatively, can you trade something, appeal to the common good, figure out some way to minimize the work—volunteering staff help, for example? Go into peer relationships with a trading mentality. To be seen as more cooperative, always explain your thinking and invite them to explain theirs. Generate a variety of possibilities first rather than stake out positions. Be tentative, allowing them room to customize the situation. Focus on common goals, priorities and problems. Invite criticism of your ideas. *More help? – See #42 Peer Relationships.*

❏ **7. Not bold enough?** Won't take a risk? Sometimes producing results involves pushing the envelope, taking chances and trying bold new initiatives. Doing those things leads to more misfires and mistakes but also better results. Treat any mistakes or failures as chances to learn. Nothing ventured, nothing gained. Up your risk comfort. Start small so you can recover more quickly. See how creative and innovative you can be. Satisfy yourself; people will always say it should have been done differently. Listen to them, but be skeptical. Conduct a postmortem immediately after finishing. This will indicate to all that you're open to continuous improvement whether the result was stellar or not. *More help? – See #2 Dealing with Ambiguity, #14 Creativity, #28 Innovation Management, and #57 Standing Alone.*

❏ **8. Procrastinate?** Are you a lifelong procrastinator? Do you perform best in crises and impossible deadlines? Do you wait until the last possible moment? If you do, you will miss deadlines and performance targets. You might not produce consistent results. Some of your work will be marginal because you didn't have the time to do it right. You settled for a "B" when you could have gotten an "A" if you had one more day to work on it. Start earlier. Always do 10% of each task immediately after it is assigned so you can better gauge what it is going to take to finish the rest. Divide tasks and assignments into thirds and schedule time to do them spaced over the delivery period. Always leave more time than you think it's going to take. *More help? – See #47 Planning and #62 Time Management.*

❏ **9. Persistence?** Perseverance? Are you prone to give up on tough or repetitive tasks, have trouble going back the second and third time, lose motivation when you hit obstacles? Trouble making that last push to get it over the top? Attention span is shorter than it needs to be? Set mini-deadlines. Break down the task into smaller pieces so you can view your progress more clearly. Switch approaches. Do something totally different next time. Have five different ways to get the same outcome. Be prepared to do them all when obstacles arise. Task trade with someone who has your problem. Work on each other's tasks. *More help? – See #43 Perseverance.*

❏ **10. The stress and strain.** Producing results day after day, quarter after quarter, year after year is stressful. Some people are energized by moderate stress. They actually work better. Some people are debilitated by stress. They decrease in productivity as stress increases. Are you close to burnout? Dealing with stress and pressure is a known technology. Stress and pressure are actually in your head, not in the outside world. Some people are stressed by the same events others are energized by—losing a major account. Some people cry and some laugh at the same external event—someone slipping on a banana peel. Stress is how you look at events, not the events themselves. Dealing more effectively with stress involves reprogramming your interpretation of your work and about what you

4

find stressful. There was a time in your life when spiders and snakes were life threatening and stressful to you. Are they now? Talk to your boss or mentor about getting some relief if you're about to crumble. Maybe this job isn't for you. Think about moving back to a less stressful job. *More help? – See #6 Career Ambition and #11 Composure.*

> *What we think or what we believe is, in the end, of little consequence. The only thing of consequence is what we do.*
> – John Ruskin, English art critic and historian

SUGGESTED READINGS

Bellman, Geoffrey M. *Getting Things Done When You Are Not in Charge*. San Francisco: Berrett-Koehler Publishers, Inc., 2001.

Block, Peter. *The Answer to How Is Yes: Acting On What Matters*. San Francisco: Berrett-Koehler Publishers, Inc., 2001.

Bossidy, Larry, Ram Charan and Charles Burck (Contributor). *Execution: The Discipline of Getting Things Done*. New York: Crown Business Publishing, 2002.

Carrison, Dan. *Deadline! How Premier Organizations Win the Race Against Time*. New York: AMACOM, 2003.

Hammer, Michael. *The Agenda: What Every Business Must Do to Dominate the Decade*. New York: Crown Business Publishing, 2001.

Hickman, Craig, Craig Bott, Marlon Berrett and Brad Angus. *The Fourth Dimension; The Next Level of Personal and Organizational Achievement*. New York: John Wiley & Sons, Inc., 1996.

Hill, Linda A. *Becoming a Manager: How New Managers Master the Challenges of Leadership*. New York: Harvard Business School Press, 2003.

Holland, Winford E. "Dutch." *Change Is the Rule: Practical Actions for Change: On Target, on Time, on Budget*. Chicago: Dearborn Trade Publishing, 2000.

Hutchings, Patricia J. *Managing Workplace Chaos: Solutions for Handling Information, Paper, Time, and Stress*. New York: AMACOM, 2002.

Lester, Richard K. *The Productive Edge: How U.S. Industries Are Pointing the Way to a New Era of Economic Growth*. New York: W.W. Norton, 1998.

Loehr, Jim and Tony Schwartz. *The Power of Full Engagement: Managing Energy, Not Time, Is the Key to High Performance and Personal Renewal*. New York: The Free Press, 2003.

Niven, P.R. *Balanced Scorecard Step-by-Step: Maximizing Performance and Maintaining Results*. New York: John Wiley & Sons, Inc., 2002.

Panella, Vince. *The 26 Hour Day: How to Gain at Least Two Hours a Day With Time Control*. Franklin Lakes, NJ: Career Press, 2002.

Pickering, Peg and Jonathan Clark. *How to Make the Most of Your Workday*. Franklin Lakes, NJ: Career Press, 2001.

Sapadin, Linda with Jack Maguire. *It's About Time! The Six Styles of Procrastination and How to Overcome Them*. New York: Viking Press, 1996.

Whipp, Richard, Barbara Adam and Ida Sabelis (Eds.). *Making Time: Time and Management in Modern Organizations*. Oxford, UK: Oxford University Press, 2002.

82. TIMELINESS OF DELIVERY OF OUTPUT

Be willing to make decisions. That's the most
important quality in a good leader. Don't fall victim
to what I call the "ready-aim-aim-aim-aim syndrome."
– T. Boone Pickens, President, Mesa Petroleum Company

General Definition: Timely delivery of goods and services in terms of schedules, deadlines, goals and targets without regard to other factors like quality and resourcefulness.

UNSKILLED
- ❏ Always among the last to finish
- ❏ Misses important deadlines by a significant amount and barely meets standard for others
- ❏ Among the slowest people or groups around

    Select one to three of the competencies listed below to use as a substitute for this Performance Management Dimension if you decide not to work on it directly.

    SUBSTITUTES: 1,2,12,17,18,20,32,37,43,50,51,52,53,62

AVERAGE
- ❏ Produces most work on time
- ❏ Timeliness is acceptable and at standard
- ❏ Meets deadlines on most work; may miss on a few
- ❏ About as timely as most other people or groups

SKILLED
- ❏ Always the first or among the first to finish
- ❏ Even unreasonable or difficult time targets and goals are met and some are actually exceeded
- ❏ Sets the speed standard for the rest

OVERUSED SKILL
- ❏ So committed to meeting deadlines and getting things done on time that things get too intense
- ❏ As the delivery target comes closer, things like quality or costs or morale suffer at the last minute
- ❏ Getting it done on time becomes too important

Select one to three of the competencies listed below to work on to compensate for an overuse of this skill.

COMPENSATORS: 11,17,23,33,36,37,39,41,42,50,52

SOME CAUSES

- ☐ Can't say no
- ☐ Disorganized
- ☐ Doesn't delegate
- ☐ Doesn't set priorities
- ☐ Not focused
- ☐ Not resourceful
- ☐ Perfectionist
- ☐ Procrastinator
- ☐ Rejects help
- ☐ Slow to make decisions
- ☐ Won't contest deadlines

THE MAP

Second in importance only to producing results is producing them on time. No one is ever performing in a vacuum. Everyone's work is just a step in a bigger chain of tasks and work. The results picture is only as good as the weakest link in the productivity chain. If your project or report or service is a day late, everyone past you will feel the pain. All beyond you will have to change their expectations and schedule. Being late will always cause frustration and irritation of all of the people down the work chain. Being timely, even sometimes at the expense of completeness or even quality, is a key virtue in today's fast-paced world. As Woody Allen says, "Being there on time is half of life."

SOME REMEDIES

☐ **1. Perfectionist?** Need or prefer or want to be 100% sure? Want to make sure that all or at least most of your decisions are right? A lot of people prefer that. Perfectionism is tough to let go of because most people see it as a positive trait for them. They pride themselves on never being wrong. Recognize perfectionism for what it might be—collecting more information than others do to improve confidence in making a fault-free decision and thereby avoiding the risk and criticism that would come from making decisions faster. Anyone with a brain, unlimited time and 100% of the data can make good decisions. The real test is who can act the soonest, being right the most, with less than all the data. Some studies suggest even successful general managers are about 65% correct. If you need to be more timely, you need to reduce your own internal need for data and the need to be perfect. Try to decrease your need for data and your need to be right all the time slightly every week until you reach a more reasonable balance between thinking it through and taking action. Try making some small decisions on little or no data. Trust your intuition more. Your experience won't let you stray too far. Let your brain do the calculations.

❏ **2. Procrastinator?** Are you a procrastinator? Get caught short on deadlines? Do it all at the last minute? Not only will you not be timely, your decision quality and accuracy will be poor. Procrastinators miss deadlines and performance targets. If you procrastinate, you might not produce consistent decisions. Start earlier. Always do 10% of thinking about the decision immediately after it is assigned so you can better gauge what it is going to take to finish the rest. Divide decisions into thirds or fourths and schedule time to work on them spaced over the delivery period. Remember one of Murphy's Laws: It takes 90% of the time to do 90% of the project, and another 90% of the time to finish the remaining 10%. Always leave more time than you think it's going to take. Set up checkpoints for yourself along the way. Schedule early data collection and analysis. Don't wait until the last moment. Set an internal deadline one week before the real one. *More help? – See #47 Planning.*

❏ **3. Disorganized?** Don't always get to everything on time? Forget deadlines? Lose requests for decisions? Under time pressure and increased uncertainty, you have to put the keel in the water yourself. You can't operate helter-skelter and make quality timely decisions. You need to set tighter priorities. Focus more on the mission-critical few decisions. Don't get diverted by trivial work and other decisions. Get better organized and disciplined. Keep a decision log. When a decision opportunity surfaces, immediately log it along with the ideal date it needs to be made. Plan backwards to the work necessary to make the decision on time. If you are not disciplined in how you work and are sometimes late making decisions and taking action because of it, buy books on TQM, ISO and Six Sigma. Go to one workshop on efficient and effective work design. *More help? – See #50 Priority Setting, #52 Process Management, #62 Time Management and #63 Total Work Systems (e.g., TQM/ISO/Six Sigma).*

❏ **4. Too cautious and conservative?** Analysis paralysis? Break out of your examine-it-to-death and always-take-the-safest-path mode and just do it. Increasing timeliness will increase errors and mistakes but it also will get more done faster. Develop a more philosophical stance toward failure/criticism. After all, most innovations fail, most proposals fail, most change efforts fail, anything worth doing takes repeated effort. The best tack when confronted with a mistake is to say, "What can we learn from this?" Ask yourself if your need to be cautious matches the requirements for speed and timeliness of your job. *More help? – See #45 Personal Learning.*

❏ **5. Stress and conflict under time pressure.** Some are energized by time pressure. Some are stressed by time pressure. It actually slows us down. We lose our anchor. We are not at our best when we are pushed. We get more anxious, frustrated, upset. Does time pressure bring out your emotional response? Write down why you get anxious under time pressure. What fears does it surface? Don't want to make a mistake? Afraid of the unknown consequences? Don't have the confidence to decide? When you get stressed, drop the problem for a moment. Go do something else. Come back to it when you are under better control. Let your brain work on it while you do something safer. *More help? – See #11 Composure and #107 Lack of Composure.*

❏ **6. Don't like risk?** Sometimes taking action involves pushing the envelope, taking chances and trying bold new initiatives. Doing those things leads to more misfires and mistakes. Research says that successful executives have made more mistakes in their careers than those who aren't successful. Treat any mistakes or failures as chances to learn. Nothing ventured, nothing gained. Up your risk comfort. Start small so you can recover more quickly. Go for small wins. Don't blast into a major task to prove your boldness. Break it down into smaller tasks. Take the easiest one for you first. Then build up to the tougher ones. Review each one to see what you did well and not well, and set goals so you'll do something differently and better each time. End up accomplishing the big goal and taking the bold action. Challenge yourself. See how creative you can be in taking action a number of different ways. *More help? – See #2 Dealing with Ambiguity, #14 Creativity, and #28 Innovation Management.*

❏ **7. Set better priorities.** You may not have the correct set of priorities. Some people take action but on the wrong things. Effective managers typically spend about half their time on two or three key priorities. What should you spend half your time on? Can you name five things that you have to do that are less critical? If you can't, you're not differentiating well. People without priorities see their jobs as 97 things that need to be done right now—that will actually slow you down. Pick a few mission-critical things and get them done. Don't get diverted by trivia. *More help? – See #50 Priority Setting.*

❏ **8. Afraid to get others involved?** Taking action requires that you get others on board. Work on your influence and selling skills. Lay out the business reason for the action. Think about how you can help everybody win with the action. Get others involved before you have to take action. Involved people are easier to influence. Learn better negotiation skills. Learn to bargain and trade. *More help? – See #31 Interpersonal Savvy, #37 Negotiating, and #39 Organizing.*

❏ **9. Not committed?** Maybe you are giving as much to work as you care to give. Maybe you have made a life/work balance decision that leads you to a fair day's work for a fair day's pay mode of operating. No more. No less. That is an admirable decision, certainly one you can and should make. Problem is, you may be in a job where that's not enough. Otherwise people would not have given you this rating. You might want to talk to your boss to get transferred to a more comfortable job for you; one that doesn't take as much effort and require as much action initiation on your part. You may even think about moving down to the job level where your balance between quality of life and effort and hours required of you at work are more balanced.

❑ **10. Lay out the process.** Most well-running processes start out with a plan. What do I need to accomplish? What's the time line? What resources will I need? Who controls the resources—people, funding, tools, materials, support—I need? What's my currency? How can I pay for or repay the resources I need? Who wins if I win? Who might lose? Buy a flow charting and/or project planning software that does PERT and GANTT charts. Become an expert in its use. Use the output of the software to communicate your plans to others. Use the flow charts in your presentations. Nothing helps move a process along better than a good plan. It helps the people who have to work under the plan. It leads to better use of resources. It gets things done faster. It helps anticipate problems before they occur. Lay out the work from A to Z. Many people are seen as lacking because they don't write the sequence or parts of the work and leave something out. Ask others to comment on your ordering and note what's missing. *More help? – See #47 Planning and #63 Total Work Systems (e.g., TQM/ISO/Six Sigma).*

Counting time is not so important as making time count.
– James Walker

SUGGESTED READINGS

Allen, David. *Getting Things Done: The Art of Stress-Free Productivity.* New York: Penguin Books, 2003.

Bacon, Terry R. and David G. Pugh. *Winning Behavior: What the Smartest, Most Successful Companies Do Differently.* New York: AMACOM, 2003.

Bossidy, Larry, Ram Charan and Charles Burck (Contributor). *Execution: The Discipline of Getting Things Done.* New York: Crown Business Publishing, 2002.

Byfield, Marilyn. *It's Hard to Make a Difference When You Can't Find Your Keys: The Seven-Step Path to Becoming Truly Organized.* New York: Viking Press, 2003.

Carrison, Dan. *Deadline! How Premier Organizations Win the Race Against Time.* New York: AMACOM, 2003.

Collins, James C. *Turning Goals Into Results: The Power of Catalytic Mechanisms* (HBR OnPoint Enhanced Edition). Boston: Harvard Business School Press, 2000.

Emmett, Rita. *The Procrastinator's Handbook: Mastering the Art of Doing It Now.* New York: Walker & Company, 2000.

Fine, Charles H. *Clock Speed—Winning Industry Control in the Age of Temporary Advantage.* Cambridge, MA: Perseus Publishing, 1998.

Hawkins, David R. *Power vs. Force: The Hidden Determinants of Human Behavior.* Carson, CA: Hay House, 2002.

Loehr, Jim and Tony Schwartz. *The Power of Full Engagement: Managing Energy, Not Time, Is the Key to High Performance and Personal Renewal.* New York: The Free Press, 2003.

Panella, Vince. *The 26 Hour Day: How to Gain at Least Two Hours a Day With Time Control.* Franklin Lakes, NJ: Career Press, 2002.

Pfeffer, Jeffrey and Robert I. Sutton. *The Knowing-Doing Gap: How Smart Companies Turn Knowledge Into Action.* Boston: Harvard Business School Press, 2000.

Tracy, Brian. *Eat That Frog! 21 Great Ways to Stop Procrastinating and Get More Done in Less Time.* San Francisco: Berrett-Koehler Publishers, Inc., 2001.

Williams, Paul B. *Getting a Project Done on Time.* New York: AMACOM, 1996.

QUALITY OF WORK OUTPUT

It's a very funny thing about life; if you refuse to accept
anything but the best, you very often get it.
– William Somerset Maugham

General Definition: The quality of goods and services produced in terms of errors, waste and rework required to meet standards, not considering other things like timeliness or quantity.

UNSKILLED
❑ Produces work that's below the quality standard
❑ Contains notable and sloppy errors
❑ Usually requires rework before it can be used and then barely meets average minimum quality standards or specifications

Select one to three of the competencies listed below to use as a substitute for this Performance Management Dimension if you decide not to work on it directly.

SUBSTITUTES: 5,15,17,18,20,28,32,33,35,39,47,50,51,52,53,65

AVERAGE
❑ Produces work that is of reasonable quality
❑ Most is acceptable, with a few errors and rework
❑ Occasionally not quite up to standard with some waste of time or resources

SKILLED
❑ The quality of the work from this person or group is always among the best
❑ Produces work that is mostly error free the first time with little waste or redone work

OVERUSED SKILL
❑ Produces very high-quality work but perfectionism leads to lower productivity, some missed deadlines, using too many resources to finish or taking too long to get there
❑ Quality standards exceed what's reasonable

Select one to three of the competencies listed below to work on to compensate for an overuse of this skill.

COMPENSATORS: 1,2,16,39,40,51,52

SOME CAUSES

- ❏ Impatient
- ❏ Not aligned or committed
- ❏ Not customer oriented
- ❏ Not-invented-here behavior
- ❏ Not planful
- ❏ Not results oriented
- ❏ Not skilled enough
- ❏ Rejects help
- ❏ Rejects suggestions
- ❏ Stuck in the old ways
- ❏ Won't delegate

THE MAP

Things that work as expected please customers—internal or external. Doing things right, especially the first time, avoids waste, rework and the consequences of disappointment. Undershooting the expectations of the customers of your tasks, projects or services almost always will have bad downstream consequences for you and those you work with. Whatever price you save for yourself by producing or being part of producing below-standard work will just have to be redone at a higher cost than before. It will take you more time and resources in total to produce and fix your work than it would take to do it right the first time.

SOME REMEDIES

- ❏ **1. Learn the principles.** There are many sources available. Read about methods put forth by Deming, Juran, Crosby, Hammer and Champy and countless others. There are numerous conferences and workshops you can attend. It's best to get a sampling of what everybody thinks and then create your own version for your specific situation.

- ❏ **2. Be customer driven.** In a free-enterprise system, the customer is king; those who please the customer best win. The same is true with internal customers; those who please them most will win. Winners are always customer oriented and responsive. Pleasing the reasonable needs of customers is fairly straightforward. First you need to know what they want and expect; the best way to do that is to ask them; then deliver that in a timely way at a price/value that's acceptable to them. Get in the habit of meeting with your internal or external customers on a regular basis to set up a dialogue; they need to feel free to contact you about problems and you need to be able to contact them for essential information. Also, get out in front of your customers; try to anticipate their needs for your products and services before they even know about them; provide your customers with positive surprises—features they weren't expecting; delivery in a shorter time; more than they ordered. *More help? – See #15 Customer Focus.*

❏ **3. Always design your work and manage your time from the customer in, not from you out.** Your best efforts will always be determined by your customers, not you. Try not to design and arrange what you do only from your own view; always try to know and take the viewpoint of your customer first; you will always win following that rule.

❏ **4. Delegate and empower others to help design the best work flows to produce zero-defect products and services that meet the needs of your customers.** This is a known process, well documented, and available to all who wish to implement its principles. *More help? – See #35 Managing and Measuring Work and #52 Process Management.*

❏ **5. Look at your own personal work habits.** Are they designed for maximum effectiveness and efficiency? Is there room for some continuous improvement? Are you applying the principles you have learned to yourself? Remember, this is one of the major reasons why these efforts fail.

❏ **6. Think of yourself as a dissatisfied customer.** Write down all of the unsatisfactory things that have happened to you as a customer during the past month. Things like delays, orders not right, cost not as promised, phone calls not returned, cold food, bad service, inattentive clerks, out-of-stock items, etc. Would your customers report any of these problems? Then do a study of your lost customers. Find out what the three key problems were and see how quickly you can eliminate 50% of the difficulties that caused them to depart. Study your competitors' foul-ups and see what you can do to both avoid them in your own organization and make your organization more attractive. *More help? – See #15 Customer Focus.*

❏ **7. Lay out the process.** Most well-running processes start out with a plan. What do I need to accomplish? What's the time line? What resources will I need? Who controls the resources—people, funding, tools, materials, support—I need? What's my currency? How can I pay for or repay the resources I need? Who wins if I win? Who might lose? Buy a flow charting and/or project planning software that does PERT and GANTT charts. Become an expert in its use. Use the output of the software to communicate your plans to others. Use the flow charts in your presentations. Nothing helps move a process along better than a good plan. It helps the people who have to work under the plan. It leads to better use of resources. It gets things done faster. It helps anticipate problems before they occur. Lay out the work from A to Z. Many people are seen as lacking because they don't write the sequence or parts of the work and leave something out. Ask others to comment on your ordering and note what's missing. *More help? – See #47 Planning and #63 Total Work Systems (e.g., TQM/ISO/Six Sigma).*

☐ **8. Results oriented impatience.** The style that chills sound problem solving the most is the results-driven, time-short and impatient person. He/she does not take the time to define problems and tends to take the first close enough solution that comes along. Studies have shown that on average, the solution somewhere between the second and third one generated is the best. Impatient people don't wait that long. Slow down. Discipline yourself to pause for enough time to define the problem better and always think of three solutions before you pick one.

☐ **9. Asking others for input.** Many try to do too much themselves. They don't delegate, listen or ask others for input. Even if you think you have the solution, ask some others for input just to make sure. Access your network. Find someone who makes a good sounding board and talk to her/him, not just for ideas, but to increase your understanding of the problem. Or do it more formally. Set up a competition between two teams, both acting as your advisors. Call a problem-solving meeting and give the group two hours to come up with something that will at least be tried. Find a buddy group in another function or organization that faces the same or a similar problem and both of you experiment.

☐ **10. Are you organized and planful?** Can people follow what you want? Do you lay out work and tasks to be done clearly? Do you set clear goals and objectives that can guide their work? *More help? – See #35 Managing and Measuring Work and #47 Planning.*

> *To find fault is easy; to do better may be difficult.*
> – Plutarch (46-120 A.D.), Greek biographer

16

SUGGESTED READINGS

Bhote, Keki. *The Ultimate Six Sigma: Beyond Quality Experience to Total Business Excellence.* New York: AMACOM, 2002.

Brock, Richard. *Inside the Minds: Profitable Customer Relationships: The Keys to Maximizing Acquisition, Retention, and Loyalty.* Boston: Aspatore Books, 2003.

Champy, James A. *X-Engineering the Corporation: Reinventing Your Business in the Digital Age.* New York: Warner Books, 2002.

Crawford, Fred and Ryan Mathews. *The Myth of Excellence.* New York: Crown Business Publishing, 2001.

Drucker, Peter F. *The Essential Drucker: The Best of Sixty Years of Peter Drucker's Essential Writings on Management.* New York: HarperBusiness, 2003.

George, Michael L. *Lean Six Sigma for Service: How to Use Lean Speed and Six Sigma Quality to Improve Services and Transactions.* New York: McGraw-Hill, Inc., 2003.

Hammer, Michael and James A. Champy. *Reengineering the Corporation: A Manifesto for Business Revolution.* New York: HarperBusiness, 2001, rev. ed. 2003.

Harry, Mikel and Richard Schroeder. *Six Sigma.* New York: Random House, 2000.

Katzenbach, Jon R. *Peak Performance.* Watertown, MA: Harvard Business School Press, 2000.

Keen, Peter and Mark McDonald. *The eProcess Edge: Creating Customer Value & Business in the Internet Era.* McGraw-Hill Osborne Media, 2000.

Larson, Alan. *Demystifying Six Sigma: A Company-Wide Approach to Continuous Improvement.* AMACOM, 2003.

Lippitt, Mary Burner and Warren H. Schmidt. *The Leadership Spectrum: 6 Business Priorities That Get Results.* Palo Alto, CA: Davies-Black Publishing, 2002.

Loehr, Jim and Tony Schwartz. *The Power of Full Engagement: Managing Energy, Not Time, Is the Key to High Performance and Personal Renewal.* New York: The Free Press, 2003.

Merrill, Peter. *Do It Right the Second Time: Benchmarking Best Practices in the Quality Change Process.* Portland, OR: Productivity Press, 1997.

Pohlman, Randolph A., and Gareth S. Gardiner with Ellen M. Heffes. *Value Driven Management: How to Create and Maximize Value Over Time for Organizational Success.* New York: AMACOM, 2000.

Prahalad, C.K. and Venkat Ramaswamy. *The Future of Competition: Co-Creating Unique Value With Customers.* Boston: Harvard Business School Press, 2004.

83

Solomon, Robert. *The Art of Client Service.* Chicago, IL: Dearborn Financial Publishing, 2003.

Tate, Rick and Josh Stroup. *The Service Pro: Creating Better, Faster, and Different Customer Experiences.* Amherst, MA: HRD Press, 2003.

Winston, Stephanie. *Getting Out From Under: Redefining Your Priorities in an Overwhelming World.* Cambridge, MA: Perseus Publishing, 2000.

Yeh, Raymond T., Keri E. Pearlson and George Kozmetsky. *Zero Time: Providing Instant Customer Value—Every Time, All the Time!* New York: John Wiley & Sons, Inc., 2000.

84 USE OF RESOURCES

A particular shot or way of moving the ball can be a
player's personal signature, but efficiency of performance
is what wins the game for the team.
– Pat Riley, U.S. basketball coach

General Definition: The efficiency of use of time, money, materials and people to produce the required goods and services without considering other factors like timeliness or quality.

UNSKILLED

❏ Uses resources inefficiently and even with the additional resources, just meets minimum standards
❏ Usually over budget on everything or significantly over on some and on budget on others
❏ Wastes time, money, material and people's productivity

Select one to three of the competencies listed below to use as a substitute for this Performance Management Dimension if you decide not to work on it directly.

SUBSTITUTES: 5,15,17,18,20,24,32,33,35,39,47,50,51,58,59

AVERAGE

❏ Most work comes in on budget, with efficient and as planned use of materials and people
❏ Some work may come in over budget
❏ About as resourceful as most other people or groups

SKILLED

❏ Uses fewer resources in terms of time, material, money and people than almost any other group
❏ Gets more things done with less
❏ A model of resourcefulness
❏ Always or almost always comes in significantly under budget in all areas

OVERUSED SKILL

❏ Although this person or group comes in on or even below budget, sometimes this is at the price of lower quantity or quality
❏ So concerned with making or beating the budget plan that other things suffer
❏ May cut corners on costs so tight that there are problems later in the work flow

Select one to three of the competencies listed below to work on to compensate for an overuse of this skill.

COMPENSATORS: 15,17,39,42,50,52,53,63

SOME CAUSES

- ❏ Difficulty saying no
- ❏ Disorganized
- ❏ Exceeds quality standards
- ❏ Impatient
- ❏ Inexperienced
- ❏ Not planful
- ❏ Poor delegation
- ❏ Rejects help
- ❏ Rejects suggestions
- ❏ Slow decision-making

THE MAP

Most anyone can produce results on time given infinite resources. The real trick is to get things done on time with the least resources you can. The rewards eventually go to those that get more done with less. There is an ever-increasing demand on limited resources. Downsizing. Trimming costs. Being the low-cost producer. Many people and projects are competing for limited resources. Going global absorbs a lot of investment spending. Being resourceful includes realistic planning and estimating, clean goal setting and planning, smart and hard work, the efficient use of ready resources, the creative use of allied resources and the effective management of time.

SOME REMEDIES

- ❏ **1. Set goals and measures.** Nothing keeps projects on time and on budget like a goal and a measure. Set goals for the whole project and the sub-tasks. Set measures so you and others can track progress against the goals. *More help? – See #35 Managing and Measuring Work.*

- ❏ **2. Laying out the work.** Most resourcefulness starts out with a plan. What do I need to accomplish? What's the time line? What resources will I need? Who controls the resources—people, funding, tools, materials, support—I need? What's my currency? How can I pay for or repay the resources I need? Who wins if I win? Who might lose? Lay out the work from A to Z. Many people are seen as disorganized because they don't write the sequence or parts of the work and leave something out. Ask others to comment on your ordering and note what's missing.

❑ **3. Bargaining for resources.** What do I have to trade? What can I buy? What can I borrow? What do I need to trade for? What do I need that I can't pay or trade for?

❑ **4. Delegating.** Getting long, complex or multi-tracked projects done involves accomplishing a series of tasks that lead up to the whole. One clear finding in the research is that empowered people work longer and harder. People like to have control over their work, determine how they are going to do it, and have the authority to make decisions. Give away as much as possible along with the authority that goes with it. Another clear finding is to pay attention to the weakest links—usually groups or elements you have the least interface with or control over—perhaps someone in a remote location, a consultant or supplier. Stay doubly in touch with the potential weak links.

❑ **5. Manage efficiently.** Watch the budget. Plan spending carefully. Have a reserve if the unanticipated comes up. Set up a funding time line so you can track ongoing expenditures.

❑ **6. Be a student of the work flows** and processes around you at airports, restaurants, hotels, supermarkets, government services, etc. As a customer, how would you design those things differently to make them more effective and efficient? What principles would you follow? Apply those same principles to your own work.

❑ **7. More what and why, less how.** The best delegators are crystal clear on what and when, and more open on how. People are more motivated when they can determine the how for themselves. Inexperienced delegators include the hows, which turns the people into task automatons instead of an empowered and energized staff. Tell them what and when and for how long and let them figure out how on their own. Give them leeway. Encourage them to try things. Besides being more motivating, it's also more developmental for them. Add the larger context. Although knowing the context may not be necessary to get the task done, people are more motivated when they know where this task fits in the bigger picture. Take three extra minutes and tell them why this task needs to be done, where it fits in the grander scheme and its importance to the goals and objectives of the unit.

❑ **8. Manage your time efficiently.** Plan your time and manage against it. Be time sensitive. Value time. Figure out what you are worth per hour and minute by taking your gross salary plus overhead and benefits. Attach a monetary value on your time. Then ask, is this worth $56 of my time? Figure out what your three largest time wasters are and reduce them 50% by batching activities and using efficient communications like e-mail and voice mail for routine matters.

❏   **9. Others will always ask you to do more than you can do.** An important time saver is the ability to constructively say no. One technique you can use is to ask the requester which of the other things they have asked you to do would they like to cancel or delay in order to do the most recent request. That way you say both yes and no and let the requester choose.

❏   **10. Too dependent upon yourself.** Look at others' solutions more. Invite discussion and disagreement, welcome bad news, ask that people come up with the second and third solution. A useful trick is to assign issues and questions before you have given them any thought. Two weeks before you are due to decide, before you have a solution in mind, ask your people to examine the issue and report to you two days before you have to deal with it. This really motivates people and makes you look less impatient.

If you can organize your kitchen, you can organize your life.
– Louis Parrish

SUGGESTED READINGS

Allen, David. *Getting Things Done: The Art of Stress-Free Productivity.* New York: Penguin Books, 2003.

Bellman, Geoffrey M. *Getting Things Done When You Are Not in Charge.* San Francisco: Berrett-Koehler Publishers, Inc., 2001.

Cohan, Peter S. *e-Profit.* New York: AMACOM, 2000.

Holland, Winford E. "Dutch." *Change Is the Rule: Practical Actions for Change: On Target, on Time, on Budget.* Chicago: Dearborn Trade Publishing, 2000.

Hutchings, Patricia J. *Managing Workplace Chaos: Solutions for Handling Information, Paper, Time, and Stress.* New York: AMACOM, 2002.

Johnson, H. Thomas and Anders Bröms. *Profit Beyond Measure: Extraordinary Results Through Attention to Work and People.* New York: The Free Press, 2000.

Koch, Richard. *The 80/20 Principle: The Secret of Achieving More With Less.* New York: Currency/Doubleday, 1998.

Niven, P.R. *Balanced Scorecard Step-by-Step: Maximizing Performance and Maintaining Results.* New York: John Wiley & Sons, Inc., 2002.

Steinbock, Dan. *The Nokia Revolution.* New York: AMACOM, 2001.

Tichy, Noel M. and Eli Cohen. *The Leadership Engine.* New York: HarperCollins, 2002.

Williams, Paul B. *Getting a Project Done on Time.* New York: AMACOM, 1996.

Young, S. David and Stephen F. O'Byrne. *EVA and Vaue-Based Management: A Practical Guide to Implementation.* New York: McGraw-Hill, Inc., 2000.

A business exists to crea
— Peter Druc

General Definition: The extent to which the g   ed meet the
expectations of the internal and external custor

UNSKILLED

☐ Produces goods and services that don't meet the minimum standards and
expectations of internal and external customers

☐ There are steady complaints and extensive rework is necessary to keep
customers minimally happy

Select one to three of the competencies listed below to use as a substitute for this
Performance Management Dimension if you decide not to work on it directly.

SUBSTITUTES: 1,3,9,16,24,27,31,32,33,38,39,43,47,48,50,51,52,53,61,63

AVERAGE

☐ Produces goods and services that usually meet the normal standards of internal
and external customers

☐ Most customers are happy, with a few customer complaints and some rework
necessary to make all customers happy

SKILLED

☐ Produces goods and services that consistently meet and sometimes exceed the
standards and expectations of internal and external customers

☐ Always up-to-date about customer needs and expectations

☐ The feedback from customers is almost always positive

OVERUSED SKILL

☐ Gives customers too much for what the organization receives in return

☐ Overly committed to produce goods and services that consistently meet and
exceed the standards and expectations of internal and external customers

☐ Uses too many resources, loses sight of other important goals and objectives
and becomes an unreasonable advocate for customers at the expense of other
organizational values and policies

Select one to three of the competencies listed below to work on to compensate for an
overuse of this skill.

COMPENSATORS: 5,9,12,34,35,38,39,42,50,51,52,53,57,58,59

SOME CAUSES

- ❑ Arrogant, always knows better
- ❑ Defensive in the face of complaints
- ❑ Difficulty saying no
- ❑ Nervous about negotiating with customers
- ❑ Not planful or organized
- ❑ Not results oriented
- ❑ Poor interpersonal skills
- ❑ Poor listening skills
- ❑ Poor time management
- ❑ Rejects input from customers
- ❑ Shy, afraid to ask

THE MAP

In a free-enterprise system, the customer is king. Those win who consistently please internal and external customers best. Meeting customer expectations is the minimum standard. In order to do that, you would have to know, or better yet, negotiate customer expectations and standards, plan and align the resources needed to meet those expectations, and then deliver. More advanced is anticipating customer needs and expectations even before customers know about them. That involves being creative and innovative with products and services, visioning the future and delivering now. You can seldom lose by being customer focused and delivery committed.

SOME REMEDIES

❑ **1. Keep in touch.** Pleasing the reasonable needs of customers is fairly straightforward. First you need to know what they want and expect. The best way to do that is to ask them. Then deliver that in a timely way at a price/value that's justified. Find ways to keep in touch with a broad spectrum of your customers to get a balanced view: face-to-face, phone surveys, questionnaires, response cards with the products and services you render, etc.

❑ **2. Customers complain; it's their job.** Be ready for the good news and the bad news; don't be defensive; just listen and respond to legitimate criticisms and note the rest. Vocal customers will usually complain more than compliment; you need to not get overwhelmed by the negative comments; people who have positive opinions speak up less.

❑ **3. Anticipate customer needs.** Get in the habit of meeting with your internal or external customers on a regular basis to set up a dialogue; they need to feel free to contact you about problems and you need to be able to contact them for essential information. Use this understanding to get out in front of your customers; try to anticipate their needs for your products and services before they even know about them; provide your customers with positive surprises; features they weren't expecting, delivery in a shorter time, more than they ordered.

❏ **4. Put yourself in your customer's shoes.** If you were a customer of yours, what would you expect; what kind of turnaround time would you tolerate; what price would you be willing to pay for the quality of product or service you provide; what would be the top three things you would complain about? Answer all calls from customers in a timely way; if you promise a response, do it; if the time frame stretches, inform them immediately; after you have responded, ask them if the problem is fixed.

❏ **5. Think of yourself as a dissatisfied customer.** Write down all of the unsatisfactory things that have happened to you as a customer during the past month. Things like delays, orders not right, cost not as promised, phone calls not returned, cold food, bad service, inattentive clerks, out-of-stock items, etc. Are any of these things happening to your customers? Then do a study of your lost customers. Find out what the three key problems were and see how quickly you can eliminate 50% of the difficulties that caused them to depart. Study your competitor's foul-ups and see what you can do to both avoid them in your own organization and make your organization more attractive.

❏ **6. Think of yourself as a satisfied customer.** Write down all of the satisfactory things that have happened to you as a customer during the past month. What pleased you the most as a customer? Good value? On-time service? Courtesy? Returned phone calls? Are any of your customers experiencing any of these satisfactory transactions with you and your business? Study your successful customer transactions so they can be institutionalized. Then study what your competitors do well and see what you can also do to improve customer service.

❏ **7. Getting work done through others?** Some people are not good managers of others. They can produce results by themselves but do less well when the results have to come from the team. Are you having trouble getting your team to work with you to get the results you need? You have the resources and the people but things just don't run well. Maybe you do too much work yourself. You don't delegate or empower. You don't communicate well. You don't motivate well. You don't plan well. You don't set priorities and goals well. If you are a struggling manager or a first-time manager, there are well-known and documented principles and practices of good managing. Do you share credit? Do you paint a clear picture of why this is important? Is their work challenging? Do you inspire or just hand out work? Read *Becoming a Manager* by Linda A. Hill. Go to one course on management. *More help? – See #18 Delegation, #20 Directing Others, #36 Motivating Others, and #60 Building Effective Teams.*

❏ **8. More what and why, less how.** The best delegators are crystal clear on what and when, and more open on how. People are more motivated when they can determine the how for themselves. Inexperienced delegators include the hows, which turn the people into task automatons instead of an empowered and energized staff. Tell them what and when and for how long and let them figure out how on their own. Give them leeway. Encourage them to try things. Besides being more motivating, it's also more developmental for them. Add the larger context. Although knowing the context may not be necessary to get the task done, people are more motivated when they know where this task fits in the bigger picture. Take three extra minutes and tell them why this task needs to be done, where it fits in the grander scheme and its importance to the goals and objectives of the unit.

❏ **9. Listening under duress.** What if you're being criticized or attacked personally? What if people are wrong in what they are saying? The rules remain the same. You need to work on keeping yourself in a calm state when getting negative feedback. You need to shift your thinking. When getting the feedback, your only task is to accurately understand what the person is trying to tell you. It is not, at that point, to accept or refute. That comes later. Practice verbal Aikido, the ancient art of absorbing the energy of your opponent, and using it to manage him/her. Let the other side vent but don't react directly. Listen. Nod. Ask clarifying questions. But don't hit back. Don't judge. Keep him/her talking until he/she runs out of venom. Separate the person from the feedback. *See Tip #4 in #108 Defensiveness for help on responding to negative attacks that aren't true. More help? – See #12 Conflict Management.*

❏ **10. You may be seen as rigid in your values stances and unwilling to accept, or even see, those of others.** *See Overdoing #22 Ethics and Values.* Rigid stances often come from childhood and early adult experiences. You may have reduced your beliefs to rigid commandments. You need to know why you hold these values and critically examine whether they are appropriate here. Statements of belief are pronouncements—a true value holds up to action scrutiny; you can say why you hold it, how it plays out in different situations, and what happens when it conflicts with other values.

Rule 1: The customer is always right.
Rule 2: If the customer is ever wrong, reread Rule 1.
– Stew Leonard, American merchant

SUGGESTED READINGS

Bell, Chip R. and Bilijack R. Bell. *Magnetic Service*. San Francisco: Berrett-Koehler Publishers, Inc., 2003.

Blackwell, Roger and Kristina Stephan. *Customers Rule! Why the E-Commerce Honeymoon is Over and Where Winning Businesses Go From Here*. New York: Crown Business Publishing, 2001.

Branham, L. *Keeping the People Who Keep You in Business*. New York: AMACOM, 2001.

Brock, Richard. *Inside the Minds: Profitable Customer Relationships: The Keys to Maximizing Acquisition, Retention, and Loyalty*. Boston: Aspatore Books, 2003.

Buckingham, Richard A. *Customer Once, Client Forever: 12 Tools for Building Lifetime Business Relationships*. New York: Kiplinger Books, 2001.

Griffin, Jill and Michael W. Lowenstein. *Customer Winback*. San Francisco: Jossey-Bass, Inc., 2001.

Gutek, Barbara A. and Theresa Welsh. *The Brave New Service Strategy*. New York: AMACOM, 2000.

Hall, Stacey and Jan Brogniez. *Attracting Perfect Customers: The Power of Strategic Synchronicity*. San Francisco: Berrett-Koehler Publishers, Inc., 2001.

Heskett, James L., W. Earl Sasser, Jr. and Leonard A. Schlesinger. *The Service Profit Chain: How Leading Companies Link Profit and Growth to Loyalty, Satisfaction, and Value*. New York: The Free Press, 1997.

Johnson, Michael D. and Anders Gustafsson. *Improving Customer Satisfaction, Loyalty and Profit*. New York: Jossey-Bass, Inc., 2000.

Keller, Ed and Jon Berry. *The Influentials*. New York: The Free Press, 2003.

Nykamp, Melinda. *The Customer Differential*. New York: AMACOM, 2001.

Prahalad, C.K. and Venkat Ramaswamy. *The Future of Competition: Co-Creating Unique Value With Customers*. Boston: Harvard Business School Press, 2004.

Reichheld, Frederick. *Loyalty Rules*. Boston: Harvard Business School Press, 2001.

Reichheld, Frederick F. with Thomas Teal. *The Loyalty Effect: The Hidden Force Behind Growth, Profits and Lasting Value*. Boston: Harvard Business School Press, 2001.

Seybold, Patricia B., Ronni T. Marshak and Jeffrey M. Lewis. *The Customer Revolution*. New York: Crown Business Publishing, 2001.

Sobel, Andrew. *Making Rain: The Secrets of Building Lifelong Client Loyalty*. New York: John Wiley & Sons, Inc., 2003.

Solomon, Michael R. *Conquering Consumerspace.* New York: AMACOM, 2003.

Solomon, Robert. *The Art of Client Service.* Chicago, IL: Dearborn Financial Publishing, 2003.

Tate, Rick and Josh Stroup. *The Service Pro: Creating Better, Faster, and Different Customer Experiences.* Amherst, MA: HRD Press, 2003.

Thompson, Harvey. *The Customer-Centered Enterprise.* New York: McGraw-Hill, Inc., 2000.

Zaltman, Gerald. *How Customers Think.* Boston: Harvard Business School Press, 2003.

Zemke, Ron and Chip R. Bell. *Service Magic: The Art of Amazing Your Customers.* Chicago, IL: Dearborn Financial Publishing, 2003.

86 FREEDOM FROM UNPLANNED SUPPORT

*We are such lovers of self-reliance, that we excuse in a man many sins, if he will
show us a complete satisfaction in his position.*
– Ralph Waldo Emerson

General Definition: The amount and intensity of supervision and support necessary
to perform up to standard.

UNSKILLED

❑ Needs significantly more than average support and time from bosses and
others to meet minimum standards

❑ Takes more maintenance and support than most people or groups to be able
to contribute up to standard

❑ Not much time left for bosses to support other people or groups

*Select one to three of the competencies listed below to use as a substitute for this
Performance Management Dimension if you decide not to work on it directly.*

SUBSTITUTES: 1,9,12,16,27,34,37,38,39,43,47,48,50,53,57

AVERAGE

❑ Performs up to standard with the usual or reasonable amount of support, help
and guidance from bosses and others

❑ As a proportion of support and time available, takes up a fair share

SKILLED

❑ Usually performs up to standard independently

❑ Takes minimal support from bosses and other sources and needs little
unplanned guidance or help

❑ Independent, self-starting

❑ Requires much less support than most other people or groups

OVERUSED SKILL

❑ So driven to work independently that is an unreasonable loner

❑ Doesn't want any help, goes own way and works on own objectives

❑ May waste time and resources working on the wrong things or in
the wrong way

*Select one to three of the competencies listed below to work on to compensate for an
overuse of this skill.*

COMPENSATORS: 3,15,33,42,50,53,60,65

86

29

SOME CAUSES

☐ Avoids criticism
☐ Avoids making decisions
☐ Avoids risk
☐ Doesn't experiment
☐ Fear of failure
☐ Inexperienced
☐ Not bold or innovative
☐ Not self-confident
☐ Perfectionist
☐ Poor management
☐ Prefers structure

THE MAP

Performing as much on your own as you can while still meeting goals and targets is what most managers expect. With the exception of those managers who micromanage, most like to set goals and assign tasks and authority and then move on to other managerial duties, leaving the rest to the skills and power of the people to perform. Asking for help and assistance because there is a real need is expected and acceptable. Depending upon direction and support due to weaknesses in your own make-up is not. Taking up the time and resources of others to get things done at high quality and on time is reasonable and laudable. Taking up the time of others to gain personal advantage or to cover a weakness is not. Doing things on your own in the gray zone is the winning career strategy.

SOME REMEDIES

☐ **1. Selling your stand.** While some people may welcome what you say and what you do, others will go after you or even try to minimize you or the situation your stand relates to. Some will sabotage. To sell your views, keep your eyes on the prize but don't specify everything about how to get there. Give others room to maneuver. Present the outcomes, targets and goals without the how to's. Welcome ideas, good and bad. Any negative response is a positive if you learn from it. Invite criticism of what you're doing. Even though you're going it alone, you need the advice and support of others to get there. Stay away from personal clashes. *More help? – See #12 Conflict Management.*

☐ **2. Develop a philosophical stance toward being wrong or losing.** After all, most innovations fail, most proposals fail, most efforts to lead change fail. Research says that successful general managers have made more mistakes in their careers than the people they were promoted over. They got promoted because they had the guts to stand alone, not because they were always right.

30

Other studies suggest really good general managers are right about 65% of the time. Put errors, mistakes and failures on your menu. Everyone has to have some spinach for a balanced diet. Don't let the possibility of being wrong hold you back from standing alone when you believe it's right.

❑ **3. Don't like risk?** Standing alone involves pushing the envelope, taking chances and suggesting bold new initiatives. Doing those things leads to more misfires and mistakes. Treat any mistakes or failures as chances to learn. Nothing ventured, nothing gained. Up your risk comfort. Start small so you can recover more quickly. Go for small wins. Send up trial balloons. Don't blast into a major stand to prove your boldness. Break it down into smaller stands. Take the easiest one for you first. Then build up to the tougher ones. Review each one to see what you did well and not well, and set goals so you'll do something differently and better each time. Challenge yourself. See how inventive you can be in taking action a number of different ways. *More help? – See #2 Dealing with Ambiguity, #14 Creativity, and #28 Innovation Management.*

❑ **4. Taking personal responsibility.** Standing alone means taking the consequences alone, both the credit and the heat. You won't always be right so you need to just be as quick to take the blame as the credit. Just say, "Yes, you're right, my stand was wrong, sorry about that." Make it a practice to conduct postmortems immediately after milestone efforts—win or lose. This will indicate to all that you're interested in improvement and excellence whether the results are stellar or not. Don't let your missteps chill your courage to speak up, step into the breach, and stake out tough stands.

❑ **5. Leading is riskier than following.** While there are a lot of personal rewards for leading, leading puts you in the limelight. Think about what happens to political leaders and the scrutiny they face. Leaders have to be internally secure. Do you feel good about yourself? They have to please themselves first and have confidence that they are on the right track. Can you defend to a critical and impartial audience the wisdom of what you're doing? They have to accept lightning bolts from detractors. Can you take the heat? People will always say it should have been done differently. Listen to them, but be skeptical. Even great leaders are wrong sometimes. They accept personal responsibility for errors and move on to lead some more. Don't let criticism prevent you from taking the lead. Build up your heat shield. Conduct a postmortem immediately after finishing milestone efforts. This will indicate to all that you're open to continuous improvement whether the result was stellar or not.

❑ **6. Haven't found your passion to lead?** Try small things. Try some leadership roles and tasks off-work. Volunteer for a leadership role in your place of worship, school, or neighborhood. Volunteer to head a task force. Start up a credit union. Volunteer for the United Way drive. Start a softball league.

❑ **7. Too cautious and conservative?** Analysis paralysis? Break out of your examine-it-to-death and always-take-the-safest-path mode and just do it. Increasing timeliness will increase errors and mistakes but it also will get more done faster. Develop a more philosophical stance toward failure/criticism. After all, most innovations fail, most proposals fail, most change efforts fail, anything worth doing takes repeated effort. The best tack when confronted with a mistake is to say, "What can we learn from this?" Ask yourself if your need to be cautious matches the requirements for speed and timeliness of your job. *More help? – See #45 Personal Learning.*

❑ **8. Hesitate in the face of resistance and adverse reaction?** Conflict slows you down, shakes your confidence in your decision? Do you backpedal? Give in too soon? Try to make everyone happy? Do your homework first. Scope the problem, consider options, pick one, develop a rationale, then go to others. Be prepared to defend your selection; know what they will ask, what they will object to, how this decision will affect them. Listen carefully, invite criticism of your idea and revise accordingly in the face of real data. Otherwise, hold your ground.

❑ **9. Delegating.** Getting long, complex or multi-tracked projects done involves accomplishing a series of tasks that lead up to the whole. One clear finding in the research is that empowered people work longer and harder. People like to have control over their work, determine how they are going to do it, and have the authority to make decisions. Give away as much as possible along with the authority that goes with it. Another clear finding is to pay attention to the weakest links—usually groups or elements you have the least interface with or control over—perhaps someone in a remote location, a consultant or supplier. Stay doubly in touch with the potential weak links.

❑ **10. Be sensitive to the time of others.** Generally, the higher up you go or the higher up the person you are interacting with is, the less time you and he/she has. Be time efficient with others. Use as little of their time as possible. Get to it and get done with it. Give them an opportunity to open new avenues for discussion or to continue, but if they don't, say your good-byes and leave.

The man who knows it can't be done
counts the risk, not the reward.
– Elbert Hubbard

SUGGESTED READINGS

Badowski, Rosanne with Roger Gittines. *Managing Up: How to Forge an Effective Relationship With Those Above You.* New York: Currency, 2003.

Dominguez, Linda R. *How to Shine at Work.* New York: McGraw-Hill Trade, 2003.

Goleman, Daniel, Annie McKee and Richard E. Boyatzis. *Primal Leadership: Realizing the Power of Emotional Intelligence.* Boston: Harvard Business School Press, 2002.

Jackson, Paul Z. and Mark McKergow. *The Solutions Focus.* Yarmouth, ME: Nicholas Brealey Publishing, 2002.

Kotter, John P. and Dan S. Cohen. *The Heart of Change: Real-Life Stories of How People Change Their Organizations.* Boston: Harvard Business School Press, 2002.

Linsky, Martin and Ronald A. Heifetz. *Leadership on the Line: Staying Alive Through the Dangers of Leading.* Boston: Harvard Business School Press, 2002.

Thornton, Paul B. *Be the Leader, Make the Difference.* Irvine, CA: Griffin Trade Paperback, 2002.

86

87 TEAM/UNIT CONTRIBUTION

If a team is to reach its potential, each player must be willing to
subordinate his personal goals to the good of the team.
– Bud Wilkinson, U.S. football coach

General Definition: Unrelated to personal or group performance, is helpful to others in the unit or organization in getting work done or setting a tone of cooperation.

UNSKILLED

☐ Rarely helpful to the rest of the team, unit or organization in getting work done or in cooperating with anyone

☐ May chill the efforts of the larger group by hesitating to get involved or even refusing to help

☐ Withholds resources and information from the others

Select one to three of the competencies listed below to use as a substitute for this Performance Management Dimension if you decide not to work on it directly.

SUBSTITUTES: 3,12,21,27,31,33,36,38,41,42,48,60,64

AVERAGE

☐ Usually helpful to the rest of the team or other units in getting work done

☐ Will cooperate with others

☐ About as helpful as most people or groups are

SKILLED

☐ Always helpful to the rest of the team/other units

☐ Among the first to volunteer to help others succeed

☐ Will share anything if it's for the team or organization

☐ A model of sharing, caring and cooperation

OVERUSED SKILL

☐ Such a team player or players that own performance sometimes suffers

☐ Takes too much time and energy helping others succeed

☐ Sometimes runs out of time and resources for own work

Select one to three of the competencies listed below to work on to compensate for an overuse of this skill.

COMPENSATORS: 12,37,50,53,57

SOME CAUSES

- ❏ A loner
- ❏ Arrogant
- ❏ Competitive
- ❏ Defensive
- ❏ Impatient with others
- ❏ Not personally productive
- ❏ Poor communications skills
- ❏ Poor interpersonal skills
- ❏ Poor negotiation skills
- ❏ Self-centered

THE MAP

While getting your own work done is always paramount, helping others get theirs done as well can also reap rewards downstream. There is reciprocity. You scratch my back and I'll scratch yours. Even though you may not need others today, you may need them tomorrow. There is the sharing of successes. If you succeed and others on your team stumble, this doesn't really help much over time. It's more fun and rewarding to be part of a winning team. There is learning. While helping others, you can always learn something useful that will help you in the future. There is personal satisfaction. Most people feel good about themselves when they have successfully helped others. If you don't help others because you don't know how, learn. If you don't help others because you don't think you have anything to contribute, ask. If you don't help others because you want to look superior, stop.

SOME REMEDIES

- ❏ **1. Establish a common cause and a shared mindset.** A common thrust is what energizes dream teams. As in light lasers, alignment adds focus, power and efficiency. It's best to get each team member involved in setting the common vision. Establish goals and measures. Most people like to be measured. People like to have checkpoints along the way to chart their progress. Most people perform better with goals that are stretching. Again, letting the team participate in setting the goals is a plus. *More help? – See #35 Managing and Measuring Work.*

- ❏ **2. To communicate with team members, work on understanding people without judging them.** You don't have to agree; you just have to understand. To build a team, invest in their learning and education; take them on trips to customers, and give them time to think problems through. Give them the benefit of your thinking and particularly what the key objectives of an effort are. The goal is to have them say, "We did it." *More help? – See #27 Informing.*

❏ **3. Resistance to the idea of a team is best overcome by focusing on** common goals, priorities and problems, selling the logic of pulling together repeatedly, listening patiently to people's concerns, protecting people's feelings but also reinforcing the perspective of why the team is needed, inviting suggestions to reach the outcome, and showing patience toward the unconverted. Maintain a light touch. *More help? – See #13 Confronting Direct Reports.*

❏ **4. Dream teams learn how to operate effectively and efficiently.** Read *Overcoming Organizational Defenses* by Chris Argyris. Half of the book is about some of the common problems teams run into that block peak performance, and the other half offers strategies and tactics for undoing those chilling team behaviors.

❏ **5. Influencing.** Peers generally do not have power over each other. That means that influence skills, understanding, and trading are the currencies to use. Don't just ask for things; find some common ground where you can provide help. What do the peers you're contacting need? Do you really know how they see the issue? Is it even important to them? How does what you're working on affect them? If it affects them negatively, can you trade something, appeal to the common good, figure out some way to minimize the work (volunteering staff help, for example)? Go into peer relationships with a trading mentality.

❏ **6. Many times, negative personal styles get in the way of effective peer relationships.** People differ in the impression they leave. Those who leave positive impressions get more things done with peers than those who leave cold, insensitive or impersonal negative impressions. *More help? – See #3 Approachability, #31 Interpersonal Savvy, and #33 Listening.*

❏ **7. If peers see you as excessively competitive, they will cut you out of the loop** and may sabotage your cross-border attempts. To be seen as more cooperative, always explain your thinking and invite them to explain theirs. Generate a variety of possibilities first, rather than staking out positions. Be tentative, allowing them room to customize the situation. Focus on common goals, priorities and problems. Invite criticism of your ideas.

❏ **8. If peers think you lack respect for them or what they do, try to keep conflicts as small and concrete as possible.** Separate the people from the problem. Don't get personal. Don't give peers the impression you're trying to dominate or push something on them. Without agreeing or disagreeing, try on their views for size. Can you understand their viewpoint? When peers blow off steam, don't react; return to facts and the problem, staying away from personal clashes. Allow others to save face; concede small points; don't try to hit a home run every time. When a peer takes a rigid position, don't reject it. Ask why—what are the principles behind the position, how do we know it's fair, what's the theory of the case? Play out what would happen if his/her position was accepted.

❏ **9. A loner.** Do you keep to yourself? Work alone or try to? Do you hold back information? Do you parcel out information on your schedule? Do you share information to get an advantage or to win favor? Do people around you know what you're doing and why? Are you aware of things others would benefit from but you don't take the time to communicate? In most organizations, these things and things like it will get you in trouble. Organizations function on the flow of information. Being on your own and preferring peace and privacy are OK as long as you communicate things to bosses, peers and teammates that they need to know and would feel better if they knew. Don't be the source of surprises.

❏ **10. Think equity.** Relationships that work are built on equity and considering the impact on others. Don't just ask for things; find some common ground where you can provide help, not just ask for it. What does the unit you're contacting need in the way of problem solving or information? Do you really know how they see the issue? Is it even important to them? How does what you're working on affect them? If it affects them negatively and they are balky, can you trade something, appeal to the common good, figure out some way to minimize the work or other impact (volunteering staff help, for example)? *More help? – See #42 Peer Relationships.*

> *Individual commitment to a group effort—that is what makes a team work, a company work, a society work, a civilization work.*
> – Vince Lombardi, U.S. football coach

SUGGESTED READINGS

Avery, Christopher M. with Meri Aaron Walker and Erin O'Toole Murphy. *Teamwork Is an Individual Skill: Getting Your Work Done When Sharing Responsibility.* San Francisco: Berrett-Koehler Publishers, Inc., 2001.

Baker, Wayne E. *Networking Smart.* New York: Backinprint.com, 2000.

Barner, Robert W. *Team Troubleshooter.* Palo Alto, CA: Davies-Black Publishing, 2000.

Chrispeels, Janet (Ed.). *Learning to Lead Together: The Promise and Challenge of Sharing Leadership.* Thousand Oaks, CA: Sage Publications, 2004.

Katzenbach, Jon R. and Douglas K. Smith. *The Wisdom of Teams: Creating the High-Performance Organization.* New York: HarperBusiness, 2003.

Kostner, Jaclyn. *BIONIC eTeamwork.* Chicago: Dearborn Trade Publishing, 2001.

Leigh, Andrew and Michael Maynard. *Leading Your Team: How to Involve and Inspire Teams.* Yarmouth, ME: Nicholas Brealey Publishing, 2002.

Lencioni, Patrick M. *The Five Dysfunctions of a Team: A Leadership Fable.* San Francisco: Jossey-Bass, Inc., 2002.

Parker, Glenn M. *Team Players and Teamwork.* San Francisco: Jossey-Bass, Inc., 1990.

Raymond, Cara Capretta, Robert W. Eichinger and Michael M. Lombardo. *FYI for Teams.* Minneapolis, MN: Lominger International: A Korn/Ferry Company, 2001–2004.

Reid, Marie and Richard Hammersley. *Communicating Successfully in Groups: A Practical Introduction for the Workplace.* London; New York: Routledge, 2000.

Robbins, Harvey and Michael Finley. *The New Why Teams Don't Work—What Goes Wrong and How to Make It Right.* San Francisco: Berrett-Koehler Publishers, Inc., 2000.

Straus, David. *How to Make Collaboration Work: Powerful Ways to Build Consensus, Solve Problems, and Make Decisions.* San Francisco: Berrett-Koehler Publishers, Inc., 2002.

Wellins, Richard, William C. Byham and George R. Dixon. *Inside Teams.* San Francisco: Jossey-Bass, Inc., 1994.

88 PRODUCTIVE WORK HABITS

*I make no secret of the fact that I would rather
lie on a sofa than sweep beneath it. But you have
to be efficient if you're going to be lazy.*
– Shirley Conran, English journalist, designer

General Definition: The extent to which overall work style is effective and productive in terms of time management, setting objectives and priorities, and following up on commitments across a variety of work challenges.

UNSKILLED

❑ Not orderly in approach to work
❑ Works on whatever comes up, gets easily diverted into less productive tasks
❑ Follow-through is spotty
❑ Wastes a lot of energy and time due to being disorganized

Select one to three of the competencies listed below to use as a substitute for this Performance Management Dimension if you decide not to work on it directly.

SUBSTITUTES: 1,18,20,35,36,39,47,50,52,53,60,62

AVERAGE

❑ Reasonably productive and organized in setting appropriate objectives and managing time
❑ Works on appropriate priorities to get the work out
❑ Follows through most of the time

SKILLED

❑ Very productive and efficient in planning and executing work
❑ Accurately scopes out the work, creates efficient workflows and processes, and assigns resources properly
❑ Consistently outperforms most other people or groups because of excellence at planning, priority setting and execution

OVERUSED SKILL

❑ So obsessed with doing things in a planned and orderly manner that work is sometimes late or exceeds even reasonable quality standards
❑ Easily thrown off balance by the unexpected and doesn't adjust well to change

Select one to three of the competencies listed below to work on to compensate for an overuse of this skill.

COMPENSATORS: 2,32,33,40,46,51,53

SOME CAUSES

- ❏ Disorganized
- ❏ Impatient
- ❏ Lack of commitment
- ❏ Lack of focus
- ❏ Lazy
- ❏ Not interested in details
- ❏ Not planful
- ❏ Poor follow-through
- ❏ Poor time management
- ❏ Procrastinator
- ❏ Slow

THE MAP

Sound personal work habits go a long way toward making many other positive things happen. Good planning skills, including the ability to estimate time and resource requirements, will always get things off to a good start and avoid having to plan later on the fly. Good goal-setting skills set the standard against which decision making and resource allocation are made easier. Time management is golden. People never have enough time so the management of your and other people's time is a key skill. Follow-through saves the day. It gives you the data necessary to check the quality of your work and make the necessary adjustments before damage is done. These are lifelong habits that affect everything you do and can always use improvement.

SOME REMEDIES

❏ **1. Lay out tasks and work.** Most successful projects begin with a good plan. What do I need to accomplish? What are the goals? What's the time line? What resources will I need? How many of the resources do I control? Who controls the rest of the resources—people, funding, tools, materials, support—I need? Lay out the work from A to Z. Many people are seen as lacking a plan because they don't write down the sequence or parts of the work and leave something out. Ask others to comment on ordering and what's missing. *More help? – See #52 Process Management and #63 Total Work Systems (e.g., TQM/ISO/Six Sigma).*

❏ **2. Watch out for the activity trap.** John Kotter, in *The General Managers*, found that effective managers spent about half their time working on one or two key priorities—priorities they described in their own terms, not in terms of what the business/organizational plan said. Further, they made no attempt to work as much on small but related issues that tend to add up to lots of activity. So rather than consuming themselves and others on 97 seemingly urgent and related

88

42

smaller activities, they always returned to the few issues that would gain the most mileage long term.

❏ **3. Set goals and measures.** Nothing keeps projects on time and on budget like a goal, a plan and a measure. Set goals for the whole project and the sub-tasks. Plan for all. Set measures so you and others can track progress against the goals. *More help? – See #35 Managing and Measuring Work.*

❏ **4. Manage efficiently.** Plan the budget and manage against it. Spend carefully. Have a reserve if the unanticipated comes up. Set up a funding time line so you can track ongoing expenditures against plan.

❏ **5. Set up a process to monitor progress against the plan.** How would you know if the plan is on time? Could you estimate time to completion or percent finished at any time? Give progress feedback as you go to people involved in implementing the plan.

❏ **6. Lay out the process.** Most well-running processes start out with a plan. What do I need to accomplish? What's the time line? What resources will I need? Who controls the resources—people, funding, tools, materials, support—I need? What's my currency? How can I pay for or repay the resources I need? Who wins if I win? Who might lose? Buy a flow charting and/or project planning software that does PERT and GANTT charts. Become an expert in its use. Use the output of the software to communicate your plans to others. Use the flow charts in your presentations. Nothing helps move a process along better than a good plan. It helps the people who have to work under the plan. It leads to better use of resources. It gets things done faster. It helps anticipate problems before they occur. Lay out the work from A to Z. Many people are seen as lacking because they don't write the sequence or parts of the work and leave something out. Ask others to comment on your ordering and note what's missing. *More help? – See #47 Planning and #63 Total Work Systems (e.g., TQM/ISO/Six Sigma).*

❏ **7. Getting work done through others?** Some people are not good managers of others. They can produce results by themselves but do less well when the results have to come from the team. Are you having trouble getting your team to work with you to get the results you need? You have the resources and the people but things just don't run well. Maybe you do too much work yourself. You don't delegate or empower. You don't communicate well. You don't motivate well. You don't plan well. You don't set priorities and goals well. If you are a struggling manager or a first-time manager, there are well-known and documented principles and practices of good managing. Do you share credit? Do you paint a clear picture of why this is important? Is their work challenging? Do you inspire or just hand out work? Read *Becoming a Manager* by Linda A. Hill. Go to one course on management. *More help? – See #18 Delegation, #20 Directing Others, #36 Motivating Others, and #60 Building Effective Teams.*

88

❏ **8. Manage your time efficiently.** Plan your time and manage against it. Be time sensitive. Value time. Figure out what you are worth per hour and minute by taking your gross salary plus overhead and benefits. Attach a monetary value on your time. Then ask, is this worth $56 of my time? Figure out what your three largest time wasters are and reduce them 50% by batching activities and using efficient communications like e-mail and voice mail for routine matters.

❏ **9. Create more time for yourself.** Taking time to plan and set priorities actually frees up more time later, rather than just diving into things, hoping that you can get them done on time. Most people out of time claim they didn't have the time to plan their time. In the Stephen Covey *Seven Habits of Highly Successful People* sense, it's sharpening your saw.

❏ **10. Not committed?** Maybe you are giving as much to work as you care to give. Maybe you have made a life/work balance decision that leads you to a fair day's work for a fair day's pay mode of operating. No more. No less. That is an admirable decision, certainly one you can and should make. Problem is, you may be in a job where that's not enough. Otherwise people would not have given you this rating. You might want to talk to your boss to get transferred to a more comfortable job for you; one that doesn't take as much effort and require as much action initiation on your part. You may even think about moving down to the job level where your balance between quality of life and the effort and hours required of you at work are more balanced.

It is better to have a bad plan than no plan at all.
– Charles De Gaulle

SUGGESTED READINGS

Allen, David. *Getting Things Done: The Art of Stress-Free Productivity.* New York: Penguin Books, 2003.

Bellman, Geoffrey M. *Getting Things Done When You Are Not in Charge.* San Francisco: Berrett-Koehler Publishers, Inc., 2001.

Block, Peter. *The Answer to How Is Yes: Acting On What Matters.* San Francisco: Berrett-Koehler Publishers, Inc., 2001.

Bossidy, Larry, Ram Charan and Charles Burck (Contributor). *Execution: The Discipline of Getting Things Done.* New York: Crown Business Publishing, 2002.

Champy, James A. *X-Engineering the Corporation: Reinventing Your Business in the Digital Age.* New York: Warner Books, 2002.

Collins, James C. *Turning Goals Into Results: The Power of Catalytic Mechanisms* (HBR OnPoint Enhanced Edition). Boston: Harvard Business School Press, 2000.

Gleeson, Kerry. *The Personal Efficiency Program: How to Get Organized to Do More Work in Less Time* (3rd ed.). New York: John Wiley & Sons, Inc., 2003.

Hutchings, Patricia J. *Managing Workplace Chaos: Solutions for Managing Information, Paper, Time, and Stress.* New York: AMACOM, 2002.

Liker, Jeffrey K. *Becoming Lean: Inside Stories of U.S. Manufacturers.* Portland, OR: Productivity Press, 1998.

Niven, P.R. *Balanced Scorecard Step-by-Step: Maximizing Performance and Maintaining Results.* New York: John Wiley & Sons, Inc., 2002.

Strebel, Paul (Ed.). *Focused Energy: Mastering Bottom-Up Organization.* New York: John Wiley & Sons, Inc., 2000.

Williams, Paul B. *Getting a Project Done on Time.* New York: AMACOM, 1996.

88

88

ADDING SKILLS AND CAPABILITIES

I never let my schooling interfere with my education.
– Mark Twain

General Definition: The extent to which any capabilities were added to the current portfolio of skills, attitudes and knowledge in order to get work done and build for the future.

UNSKILLED

❏ Shows little interest in learning and building new skills and knowledge
❏ Stuck in a comfort zone—getting out of date
❏ Appears content with skills as they are

Select one to three of the competencies listed below to use as a substitute for this Performance Management Dimension if you decide not to work on it directly.

SUBSTITUTES: 1,6,18,19,32,33,44,45,54,55,61

AVERAGE

❏ Has about as much interest in learning new skills and knowledge as others do
❏ If it fits in with the work, will learn when the opportunity is there
❏ Generally keeps up with near-term new skill requirements

SKILLED

❏ Eagerly learns new skills and capabilities to improve for the future
❏ Makes learning new skills and capabilities a high priority
❏ More and better skilled at the end of the year than at the beginning

OVERUSED SKILL

❏ Spends so much time skill building that doesn't focus enough on day-to-day work
❏ Sometimes works on new skills that turn out to be only marginally helpful later

Select one to three of the competencies listed below to work on to compensate for an overuse of this skill.

COMPENSATORS: 1,16,17,32,50,51,53,58

SOME CAUSES

❏ Avoids criticism
❏ Comfortable with what is

continued

❑ Doesn't admit to shortcomings
❑ Doesn't set forward priorities
❑ Low self-awareness
❑ Not a risk taker
❑ Not career oriented
❑ Not future oriented
❑ Procrastinator
❑ Too busy

THE MAP

It's hard enough to be totally prepared for today much less spend time and energy getting ready for tomorrow. But, there is no rest for the career-minded individual. At the pace the world is moving, anticipating the knowledge and skill requirements on your path to where you want to go is essential. Jobs are getting more demanding and requiring higher-level skills. Technology is exploding. Information is more available to all. Speed is increasing. There is no option. You have to block out time to keep up and more importantly get ahead of the career curve.

SOME REMEDIES

❑ **1. Many people don't know how careers are built.** Most are put off by the popular myth of getting ahead. All of us have seen *How to Succeed in Business Without Really Trying* or something like it. It's easy to get cynical and believe that successful people are political or sell out, suck up, knife people in the back, it's who you know, and so on. The facts are dramatically different from this. Those behaviors get people in trouble eventually. What has staying power is performing and problem solving on the current job, having a few notable strengths, and seeking new tasks you don't know how to do. It's solving every problem with tenacity while looking for what you haven't yet done and getting yourself in a position to do it. Read *The Lessons of Experience* by McCall, Lombardo and Morrison for the careers of men and *Breaking the Glass Ceiling* by Morrison, White and Van Velsor for the careers of women to see how successful careers really happen.

❑ **2. Break out of your career comfort zone.** Maybe you haven't seen enough. Pick some activities you haven't done before but might find exciting. Take a course in a new area. Task trade—switch tasks with a peer. Volunteer for task forces and projects that are multi-functional or multi-business in nature. Read more broadly. *More help? – See #46 Perspective.*

❑ **3. Don't know what it takes?** Think of five successful people in your organization/field whom you know well and ask what drives them? What sorts of jobs have they held? What are their technical skills? Behavioral skills? Use the

LEADERSHIP ARCHITECT® Sort Cards to determine what the 10 key skills of each person are; compare this list with your own self-assessment and feedback. Ask Human Resources if they have a success profile for some of the jobs you may be interested in. Make a list of what you need to work on next.

❑ **4. Not willing to make sacrifices?** Many people turn down career opportunities based upon current life comforts only to regret it later when they have been passed by. Studies indicate that the vast majority of moves successful general managers had to make during their careers were not seen as right for them at the time. They tried to turn them down. We all have the problems. Children in school. A house we like. A parent to take care of. A working spouse. A medical issue to manage. A good neighborhood. Most successful careers require moving around during the years that are the most inconvenient and painful—when we have kids in school, not much extra money, and aging parents to manage. Read *The Lessons of Experience* by McCall, Lombardo and Morrison for the careers of men and *Breaking the Glass Ceiling* by Morrison, White and Van Velsor for the careers of women to see how successful careers are really built. Set your mind to it. You must move to grow.

❑ **5. Assessment.** First, get a good multi-source assessment, a 360° questionnaire, or poll 10 people who know you well to give you detailed feedback on what you do well and not well, what they'd like to see you keep doing, start doing and stop doing. You don't want to waste time on developing things that turn out not to be needs.

❑ **6. Next, divide your skills into these categories**

- Clear strengths—Me at my best.
- Overdone strengths—I do too much of a good thing—"I'm so confident that I'm seen as arrogant."
- Hidden strengths—Others rate me higher than I rate myself.
- Blind spots—I rate myself higher than others rate me.
- Weaknesses—I don't do it well.
- Untested areas—I've never been involved in strategy formulation.
- Don't knows—I need more feedback.

❑ **7. What's important?** Find out what's important for your current job and the two or three next jobs you might have an opportunity to get. See if there are success profiles for those jobs. Compare the top requirements with your appraisal. If there are no success profiles, ask the Human Resources Department for help or ask one or two people who now have those jobs what skills they need and use to be successful.

89

❏ **8. Show others you take your development seriously.** State your developmental needs and ask for their help. Research shows that people are much more likely to help and give the benefit of the doubt to those who admit their shortcomings and try to do something about them. They know it takes courage. *More help? – See #44 Personal Disclosure.*

❏ **9. Arrogance is a major blockage to self-knowledge.** Many people who have a towering strength or lots of success get little feedback and roll along until their careers get in trouble. If you are viewed as arrogant, you may have to repeatedly ask for feedback, and when you get it, there may be some anger with it. Almost by definition, arrogant people overrate themselves in the eyes of others. Others who think you are arrogant might rate you lower than neutral observers would. If you devalue others, they will return the insult.

❏ **10. Defensiveness is the other major blockage to self-knowledge.** Here people suspect you really can't take it, that you are defending against something, probably by blaming it on others or the job context. Defensive people get less feedback, thereby fulfilling their dream of being perfect. To break this cycle, you will need to follow the rules of good listening *(More Help – See #33 Listening)* and give examples of the behavior being described to validate what people are saying. This may sound unfair, but you should initially accept all feedback as accurate, even when you know it isn't. On those matters that really count, you can go back and fix it later. *More help? – See #108 Defensiveness.*

Experience is one thing you can't get for nothing.
– Oscar Wilde

SUGGESTED READINGS

Bell, Arthur H., Ph.D. and Dayle M. Smith, Ph.D. *Motivating Yourself for Achievement.* Upper Saddle River, NJ: Prentice Hall, 2002.

Bolles, Richard N. *What Color Is Your Parachute? 2006: A Practical Manual for Job-Hunters & Career-Changers.* Berkeley, CA: Ten Speed Press, 2006.

Brim, Gilbert. *Ambition: How We Manage Success and Failure Throughout Our Lives.* New York: Backinprint.com, 2000.

Champy, James and Nitin Nohria. *The Arc of Ambition.* Cambridge, MA: Perseus Publishing, 2000.

Christian, Ken. *Your Own Worst Enemy: Breaking the Habit of Adult Underachievement.* New York: Regan Books, 2004.

Glickman, Rosalene. *Optimal Thinking: How to Be Your Best Self.* New York: John Wiley & Sons, Inc., 2002.

Handy, Charles B. *21 Ideas for Managers: Practical Wisdom for Managing Your Company and Yourself.* San Francisco: Jossey-Bass, Inc., 2000.

Holton, Bil and Cher Holton. *The Manager's Short Course. Thirty-Three Tactics to Upgrade Your Career.* New York: John Wiley & Sons, Inc., 1992.

Lombardo, Michael M. and Robert W. Eichinger. *The Leadership Machine.* Minneapolis, MN: Lominger International: A Korn/Ferry Company, 2001–2006.

Maslow Abraham Harold and Deborah C. Stephens, (Ed.) and *The Maslow Business Reader.* New York: John Wiley & Sons, Inc., 2000.

McCall, Morgan W., Michael M. Lombardo and Ann M. Morrison. *The Lessons of Experience.* Lexington, MA: Lexington Books, 1988.

Morrison, Ann M., Randall P. White, Ellen Van Velsor and the Center for Creative Leadership. *Breaking the Glass Ceiling: Can Women Reach the Top of America's Largest Corporations?* Reading, MA: Addison-Wesley Publishing Company, 1992.

Niven, David. *The 100 Simple Secrets of Successful People: What Scientists Have Learned and How You Can Use It* (2nd ed.). New York: HarperBusiness, 2006.

Pirsig, Robert M. *Zen and the Art of Motorcycle Maintenance.* New York: Bantam Books, 1984.

Prochaska, James O., John C. Norcross and Carlo C. DiClemente. *Changing for Good.* New York: Avon Books, 1995.

Stone, Florence M. and Randi T. Sachs. *The High-Value Manager—Developing the Core Competencies Your Organization Needs.* New York: AMACOM, 1995.

89

90 ALIGNMENT AND COMPLIANCE: WALKING THE TALK

Buddha left a road map, Jesus left a road map, Krishna
left a road map, Rand McNally left a road map.
But you still have to travel the road yourself.
– Stephen Levine

General Definition: The extent to which this person behaves in a way that is aligned with the values, culture and mission of the organization without regard to how well they do their work.

UNSKILLED
❑ Thinks he/she has a better way
❑ Clashes with the organizational culture
❑ Mostly out of line with culture, values and mission
❑ May be a maverick
❑ Doesn't understand the right way

Select one to three of the competencies listed below to use as a substitute for this Performance Management Dimension if you decide not to work on it directly.

SUBSTITUTES: 2,3,4,11,17,22,26,29,31,40,41,48,53

AVERAGE
❑ Reasonable alignment with culture, values and mission
❑ Generally behaves in line with common organizational practices

SKILLED
❑ Is aligned with the culture, values and mission
❑ Operates with the mission and values in mind
❑ Encourages others to act in a manner aligned with organizational culture, values and mission

OVERUSED SKILL
❑ So dedicated to doing things the organization's way that judgment gets clouded
❑ Can only see things through the filter of organizational values, culture and mission
❑ So compliant that risk-taking and innovation stall
❑ Has trouble seeing when exceptions need to be made

90

Select one to three of the competencies listed below to work on to compensate for an overuse of this skill.

COMPENSATORS: 1,14,15,17,21,28,32,33,34,40,45,46,48,51,55,64

SOME CAUSES

☐ A loner
☐ Doesn't like rules and traditions
☐ Resists authority
☐ Enjoys being different
☐ Considers organizational traditions and mores a waste of his/her time
☐ Thinks the job and the business is all that matters
☐ Lacks ethics; Machiavellian

THE MAP

Culture is the glue that holds organizations together. With it, people understand what to do in a variety of situations where specific policies and practices do not exist. Standards for treatment of others and customers are widely known and accepted. Without a strong culture, inconsistency is the norm. Practices vary widely from unit to unit—one may be quite customer-focused, while the next treats customers as transactions to be dispensed with as quickly as possible. Strong cultures attract people who enjoy acting as the organization wants them to and who believe in the mission and values of the organization.

SOME REMEDIES

☐ **1. Be part of the loyal (and quiet) opposition.** Assuming you are part of this organization voluntarily, aside from getting a job, you signed on for what goes with it—a culture, norms, rules of behavior, preferred ways of doing things, and values. You can't have one without the other. Most organizations take these things quite seriously. Many times they are in the annual report and hung from the walls in the building. There is the formal organization with visible and mostly known values and rules of conduct and the informal organization where things are less often expressed and more assumed to be understood. In some organizations, the formal and informal are matched, but in others there is a gap between stated and below-the-surface values and rules. While with this organization, it's your responsibility to reasonably conform to what's expected, assuming it doesn't violate your personal or public ethics and laws. It's best to stay quiet about your differences (be part of the loyal opposition) in informal and public settings. On the other hand, feel free to express your concerns in settings conducive to open debate and honest differences of opinion. It's best if your motive is the improvement of the organization rather than your personal preferences.

06

❏ **2. Do you really understand?** In order to oppose a set of rules of conduct, norms, standards of behavior, or values, you need to understand them. First, where did they come from? What's the history? The day the company was founded? Carved on an oak tree next to the original building? Formed after a big event? The result of litigation? Borrowed from another organization (merger or acquisition)? Second, what are they designed to do? If everyone really did all these things the right way, what would the outcome be? Is there anything negative that would happen? Third, who are the current caretakers? The top person? Top management? The entire organization? Fourth, who knows the most about them? The corporate counsel? A very long-service senior executive? HR? Your boss? Go to the sources to learn about what you think you have a problem with. Armed with as complete knowledge as is available, if you are still troubled, follow the other tips.

❏ **3. Downsizing the gap.** Almost all gaps and conflicts over rules of conduct, norms and values have some common points that get lost in the heat of the battle. When a conflict happens, start by saying that it might be helpful to see if we agree on anything. Write them on the flip chart. Focus on common goals, priorities, and problems. Then write down the areas left open. Keep the open conflicts as small as possible and concrete. The more abstract it gets, "I don't think honest people would act that way," the more unmanageable it gets. Instead, be very specific with real-life examples of what you would think is better, why, and what might be the improved outcomes. Usually after calm discussion, the gap narrows. That's easier to deal with. Allow others to save face by conceding small points that are not central to your issue, and don't try to hit a home run every time. If you can't agree on a solution, agree on a procedure to move forward. Collect more evidence and arguments. Appeal to a higher power. Get a third party arbitrator. This creates some positive motion and breaks stalemates.

❏ **4. Causing unnecessary noise.** Language, words, and timing set the tone and can cause unnecessary conflict that has to be managed before you can get anything done. Do you use insensitive language? Do you raise your voice often? Do you use terms and phrases that challenge others? Do you use demeaning or dismissive terms? Do you use negative humor? Do you offer conclusions, solutions, statements, dictates, or answers too early in the discussion? Give reasons first, solutions last. When you give solutions first, people often directly challenge the solutions instead of defining the problem. Pick words that are other-person neutral. Pick words that don't challenge or sound one-sided. Pick tentative and probabilistic words that give others a chance to maneuver and save face. Pick words that are about the problem and not the person. Avoid direct blaming remarks. Describe the problem and its impact. Don't hide your thoughts and values and feelings, but don't exaggerate them either.

90

❑ **5. Too emotional or passionate about your notion of the right rules and values?** Sometimes our passion and emotional reactions lead others to think we have problems with conforming to rules and values. In those types of conflict situations, what emotional reactions do you have (such as impatience or non-verbals like flushing or drumming your pen or fingers)? Learn to recognize those as soon as they start and substitute something more neutral. Most emotional responses to conflict come from personalizing the issue. Separate people issues from the problem at hand and deal with people issues separately and later if they persist. Always return to facts and the problem before the group; stay away from personal clashes. Attack the problem by looking at common interests and underlying concerns, not people and their positions. Try on their views for size, the emotion as well as the content. Ask yourself if you understand their feelings. Ask what they would do if they were in your shoes. See if you can restate each other's position and advocate it for a minute to get inside each other's place. If you get emotional, pause and collect yourself. You are not at your best when you get emotional. Then return to the problem. *More help? – See #11 Composure and #107 Lack of Composure.*

❑ **6. Larger-scale organizational conflict.** Organizations are a complex maze of constituencies, issues, and rivalries peopled by strong egos, sensitivities, and empire protectors. Many times, larger organizations have multiple sets of rules and values depending upon what part of the organization you are in. Compliance mistakes come in a variety of shapes and sizes. The most common is saying things you shouldn't. Next are actions that are politically out of line and not right for the context. Next are unnecessary conflicts, tensions, misunderstandings, and rivalries created because you went after a specific person or group. Worst are unacceptable moves, initiatives, tactics, and strategies. Get to know your values snafus and which of the above errors you commit. Work to understand the politics of the organization. Who are the movers and shakers in the organization? Who are the major gatekeepers who control the flow of resources, information, and decisions? Who are the guides and the helpers? Get to know them better. Do lunch. Who are the major resisters and stoppers? Try to avoid or go around them or make peace with them. In the special case of dealing with top management, sensitivities are high, egos are big, sensitivity traps are set, and tensions can be severe. There is a lot of room for making statements or acting in ways that would be seen as exhibiting your lack of compliance. *More help? – See #38 Organizational Agility, #48 Political Savvy, and #119 Political Missteps.*

❑ **7. Do you act situationally?** Not everyone has a deep keel in the values water. You might just be inconsistent in your statements and actions across situations. You change your mind based on mood or who you talked with last or what your last experience was. You may express a pro people value in one instance (people you manage) and an anti people value in another (people from another unit).

You may rigidly adhere to a high moral code in one transaction—with customers, and play it close to the acceptable margin in another—with vendors. You may match your values with your audience when managing up and not when you're managing down. People are more comfortable with consistency and predictability. Do you do one thing with people you like and quite another with people you don't? Look for the three to five areas where you think these inconsistencies play out. Write down what you did with various people so you can compare. Did you do different things in parallel situations? Do you hold others to a different standard? Do you have so many value positions that they have to clash eventually? Try to balance your behavior so that you are more consistent across situations.

❏ **8. Mismatch?** At the least, a low rating for compliance means the values and ethics you are operating under are not in line with the commonly held values and ethics of those around you. That's a common problem. You join an organization thinking it has the values you believe in, and after you are there for a while, you find out they are something different. Or the organization makes a big shift in direction, gets acquired, or merges and changes its ethics and values overnight, out of your comfort zone. To some extent, that's life. It's hard to find a perfect match. If the gap is serious, leave. If the gap is just uncomfortable, try to affect it in any way you can by influencing the organization. Try not to challenge others with your discomfort. Maybe you're too independent. You set your own rules, smash through obstacles, see yourself as tough, action oriented and results oriented. You get it done. The problem is you don't often worry about whether others think as you do. You operate from your inside out. What's important to you is what you think and what you judge to be right and just. In a sense, admirable. In a sense, not smart. You live in an organization that has both formal and informal commonly held standards, beliefs, ethics, and values. You can't survive long without knowing what they are and bending yours to fit. Try to be a supporter of what you can and just be silent about the rest.

❏ **9. Do you apply double standards?** Another common problem is having one set of standards for you and a different set of standards for others. Or one set for you and the people you like and another for everyone else. Do you do what you expect others to do? Don't ask anyone to do what you wouldn't do. A common problem with higher level managers is telling the people below them to make tough people calls and fire those who don't meet standards. Then they give everyone reporting to them an above-average rating and a bonus even though everyone knows one or two of these people are not up to standard. Do you do anything like this? Do you make close calls in favor of those you like or play favorites? Try to be more consistent.

❏ **10. Don't walk your good talk?** The usual case is that there is a sizable gap between what you say about your ethics and values and what the ethics and values of others should be, and what you actually do in those same situations.

We have worked with many who get themselves in trouble by making values and ethics speeches, high-toned, inspiring, lofty, passionate, charismatic, give you goose bumps—until you watch that person do the opposite or something quite different in practice. Examine all the things you tend to say in speeches or in meetings or casual conversations that are values and ethics statements about you or what you think others should do. Write them down the left side of a legal pad. For each one, see if you can write three to five examples of when you acted exactly in line with that value or ethic. Can you write down any that are not exactly like that? If you can, it's the gap that's the problem. Either stop making values and ethics statements you can't or won't model, or bring your stated values into alignment with your own actions.

❏ **11. Don't walk your bad talk?** Another, though more rare, possibility is that there is a sizable gap between what you say and the language you use, and what you actually think and do. We have worked with some people who get themselves in trouble by using language and words that imply marginal values and ethics that make others uncomfortable. Do you shoot for effect? "Fire them all." Do you exaggerate? "There are no good vendors." Do you push your statements to the extreme to make a point? Do you overstate negative views? Do you trash talk to fit in? Do you use demeaning words? "All consultants are just mercenaries." What if I have never seen you in action? What would I think your values were if I listened to you talk and didn't know what you actually do? Examine the words and the language you tend to use in speeches or in meetings or casual conversations that are values and ethics based. Write them down the left side of a legal pad. For each one, see if you can write three to five examples of when you acted exactly in line with those words. Do you really act like that? Do you really think that way? If you don't, it's the gap that's the problem. Stop using words and language that are not in line with your real thoughts, values, and actions.

❏ **12. Are you hanging on to old values?** This is a tough one. Times change. Do values change? Some think not. That might be your problem. What about humor? Could you tell some ribald jokes ten years ago that would get you in trouble today? Using the example of sexual harassment, what is it to you? What's the difference between poor taste, kidding, flirting, and sexual harassment? Has the definition changed over your working career? Do you think your old values are better than today's? When did you form your current values? Over 20 years ago? Maybe it's time to examine your personal commandments in light of the new today to see whether you need to make any midcourse corrections. Others may view your stances as simplistic or rigid. List five common areas where values clash for you at work—such as quality/cost trade-offs, work with someone or fire, treat people differently or all the same. Can you describe how you deal with these situations? What are your tie-breakers? What wins out? Why? If you find yourself coming down on the same side in the same way almost every time, you need an update. Talk to people who would go the other way and begin to see more complexity in the issue. Turn off your judgment programming—listen to understand.

☐ **13. The worst case.** On the more negative side, it could mean you have unacceptable values and ethics; that is, most would reject them. You may operate too close to or over the edge for most people to feel comfortable with you. You hedge, sabotage others, play for advantage, set up others, and make others look bad. You may be devious and scheming and overly political. You tell yourself it's OK because you're getting results. You really believe the end justifies the means. You tell people what they want to hear and then go off and do something else. If any of this is true, this criticism should be a repeat for you. This is not something that develops overnight. You need to find out if your career with this organization is salvageable. The best way to do this is to admit that you know your ethics and values are not the same as the people you work with and ask a boss or a mentor whether it's fixable. If they say yes, contact everyone you think you've alienated and see how they respond. Tell them the things you're going to do differently. Ask them if the situation can be repaired. Longer term, you need to seek some professional counsel on your values and ethics, or find a place that has the same set as you do.

☐ **14. Adjusting your values and ethics.** Remember, behavior is ten times more important than words. What values do you want? What do you want your ethics to be? Write them down the left-hand side of the page (e.g., I want to be known as a fair manager). Then down the right side, what would someone with that value do and not do? For example, "Wouldn't play favorites"; "Would offer everyone opportunities to grow and develop"; "Would listen to everyone's ideas"; "Would call for everyone's input in a staff meeting"; "Would apportion my time so everyone gets a piece of it"; "Would hold everyone to the same standards." Have someone you trust check it over to see if you are on the right track. Then start to consistently do the things you have written on the right-hand side.

> *You get the best out of others when you give the best of yourself.*
> – Harry Firestone

SUGGESTED READINGS

Badaracco, Joseph L., Jr. *Defining Moments—When Managers Must Choose Between Right and Right.* Boston: Harvard Business School Press, 1997.

Badaracco, Joseph L., Jr. *Leading Quietly.* Boston: Harvard Business School Press, 2002.

Badaracco, Joseph L., Jr. *The Discipline of Building Character* (HBR OnPoint Enhanced Edition). Boston: Harvard Business School Press, 2002.

Deal, Terrence E. and Allan A. Kennedy. *Corporate Cultures.* Cambridge, MA: Perseus Publishing, 2000.

Dobrin, Arthur. *Ethics for Everyone: How to Increase Your Moral Intelligence.* New York: John Wiley & Sons, Inc., 2002.

Gallagher, Richard S. *The Soul of an Organization: Understanding the Values That Drive Successful Corporate Cultures.* Chicago, IL: Dearborn Financial Publishing, 2003.

Johnson, Craig E. *Meeting the Ethical Challenges of Leadership: Casting Light or Shadow* (2nd ed.). Thousand Oaks, CA: Sage Publications, 2004.

Klein, Alec. *Stealing Time: Steve Case, Jerry Levine, and the Collapse of AOL Time Warner.* New York: Simon & Schuster, 2003.

McLean, Bethany and Peter Elkind. *The Smartest Guys in the Room: The Amazing Rise and Scandalous Fall of Enron.* New York: Portfolio, 2003.

Seglin, Jeffrey L. *The Good, the Bad, and Your Business: Choosing Right When Ethical Dilemmas Pull You Apart.* New York: John Wiley & Sons, Inc., 2000.

Sonnenberg, Frank K. *Managing With a Conscience—How to Improve Performance Through Integrity, Trust and Commitment.* New York: McGraw-Hill Trade, 1996.

Tichy, Noel M. and ,Stratford Sherman. *Control Your Destiny or Someone Else Will: How Jack Welch Is Making General Electric the World's Most Competitive Corporation.* New York: HarperBusiness, 2001.

Appendix Index

APPENDIX A: JOB IMPROVEMENT STRATEGIES

Are you ready for job improvement? What is your need? How will you improve? The information that follows will help you answer these questions.

Establish the Need

The first step in improvement is awareness. Be honest with yourself. Dig deep to determine your real improvement needs. Many times you'll find there's a combination of issues that, taken together, create a significant improvement opportunity.

There are four typical conditions that indicate you might benefit from improvement:

1. You are average in a skill that is important—you need to be above average.

2. You are weak (below average) in a skill in which you need to be at least average.

3. You are untested (possibly unskilled) in an important area.

4. You overuse or overdo one of your strong skills to the point that it is causing problems for you.

Which condition(s) best describes you? Are you ready to admit that improvement is important? Is it important enough to take action? If not, there is little point in reading further. However, if you're committed to improving your job performance, go to the next steps below to complete a personal job improvement plan and get started.

Create a Personal Job Improvement Plan

1. For each Dimension, read the **Unskilled** definition and identify the bullet points that best describe you. Then, look to the **Skilled** definition and identify those aspects that you would like to describe you after improvement. Complete the before-and-after picture in your personal improvement plan in Appendix B.

2. Now, check the **Causes** that might apply to you. Many improvement efforts have floundered because the plan attacked the wrong problem. Write down your particular need—what it looks like, what causes it, who it plays out with and in what situations. If your causes aren't listed, add them to the list. In Appendix B, record your performance needs on the Some Causes form.

3. Read the **Map**. The Map gives you the lay of the land. It reviews the general case of the Performance Dimension, how it operates, and why it's important. Pay attention to the things about the Dimension you didn't understand before you read the map. Those added learnings will make a difference in your improvement plan. Record your learnings on the form in Appendix B.

A-1

4. Read the **Remedies** for information on tactics for improving in any area. Pick those that best fit your situation and needs and record them on the Performance Improvement and Action Plans form in Appendix B. These tactics can serve as a basic core for any improvement plan.

Take Action

After you've identified your need, follow one of these four strategies for each need:

1. **Improve.** Build your skills by embracing the improvement suggestions provided in the remedies.

2. **Substitute.** Apply a different skill that you do have to cover for, substitute for, or neutralize the negative effects of a skill you are lacking.

3. **Workaround.** Use any of the 10 workaround strategies discussed in this Appendix to neutralize the weakness and cover for an inadequate skill.

4. **Live with it.** Accept it. Adjust your improvement goals to reflect the reality of your skill deficiency. At least you'll be honest. Consider changing your job or intended career path to better reflect your strengths.

If You Choose to Improve

1. Look at the specific remedies listed for the Dimension and pick the ones that apply. Each remedy is a tip written to address a lack of skill. It is unlikely that all of the remedies or tips will apply to any one person. Look back to the causes you checked and what you learned from the map related to the importance of the Dimension. Investigate the cross-references to the 67 Leadership Competencies and additional remedies in Appendix F. Use the reproducible forms in Appendix B to capture your plan.

2. Lay out a plan of action and a schedule. Include at least three items you will work on immediately. Track your progress by recording the times you did or did not take action on each item. Establish a target completion date of one month or less. Take the deadline seriously. If your time frame is longer (or indefinite!), you'll be less likely to do anything. Start today.

3. There are numerous tactics you can employ to make your improvement plan more effective:

    -   **Neutralize your weaker areas.** If you have a problem with productive work habits, for instance, your first goal should be to turn this from a negative to a neutral. Start small, using the remedies and specific tips provided.

    -   **Seek further feedback.** Little happens without feedback. Get a feedback partner; get formal 360° feedback; poll people you work with about what you should keep doing, stop doing, and start doing. Modify your behavior accordingly.

- **Test the unknown.** In some Performance Dimensions you might lack experience. It's what we call an untested area. Maybe you don't work well in a team, but have little experience working in a team environment. Pick something manageable that needs doing, and give it a try using the tips.

- **Go against your natural grain.** If you naturally focus on quality but do so at the expense of speed, you'll have to work on the quantity of output more vigorously. Few succeed in a different job by simply repeating past successful behavior. This is a strong lesson from career research. You'll have to stretch in uncomfortable areas. For example, whether you gravitate toward customer focus or not, you can learn the behaviors that lead to excellent customer impact. You might even come to enjoy it. It's important not to confuse what you like to do with what's necessary to do.

- **Use jobs for improvement.**

  (a) The number one developer of competence—by far—is stretching, challenging jobs. It's not courses. It's not feedback or role models. Real jobs are where you will find the best opportunities to improve and exercise significant and varied competencies. Jobs matter most for long-term success. Extensive research by the Center for Creative Leadership shows that executives who maintain an enduring track record of success have been tested in many types of difficult jobs.

  (b) You have a rich opportunity to use your job to learn better from experience. What is it specifically about the job that demands you work on this need? Write down these challenges; focus on them.

  (c) Make use of part-time assignments. Unless you have challenging job tasks where you either perform against the need or fail, not much improvement will occur. This is the essence of action learning or learning from experience—not simulation or practice, not simply trying things out, but a genuine performance situation that requires you to get better at something. For example, consider Performance Dimension 84 related to the efficient use of resources. Now, the truth is that everyone has had many opportunities to practice frugality and conservation of resources. However, many have simply chosen to not expend the effort to reduce waste or streamline processes. To develop in this Dimension, then, how about an assignment to run a task force working on waste reduction? In this case, success would require a proactive approach to eliminating waste. Any improvement plan you write must have perform-this-or-else tasks in it to work, tasks with meaningful consequences for success and for failure. Otherwise, you'll lack sufficient motivation to change. Bad habits will prevail. Select improvement activities that have built-in consequences and shape those activities to fit your job and organization.

What tasks like these are available in your job? If you have a significant need—if you are really weak in this area—start with smaller challenges and build up to the tougher ones.

Alternatives to Skill Improvement

Use the strategies provided above to target Dimensions and related competencies for improvement. Keep in mind, however, that you don't have to be good at everything. Most successful leaders have several major strengths, but tend to lack glaring weaknesses. Improving in all is unlikely. If directly working on improvement in a particular area seems unlikely, use the indirect strategies below.

1. **Substitute.** Use strength in one Dimension to attack weakness in another. For example, let's say you frequently miss deadlines because you're slow, a perfectionist, and a procrastinator. If you look at the list of substitutes provided following the Unskilled description of Dimension 82: Timeliness of Delivery of Output, you'll find substitutes that include Conflict Management (12), Delegation (18), Directing Others (20), and Negotiating (37). If these are skills that you already have or are more inclined to develop, they can serve, at least to some extent, as a substitute for timely delivery.

2. **Work around the need.** Use other resources to get the same thing done. The goal of a workaround is to reduce the noise caused by the need. While there may or may not be any learning attached to the workaround, it will get you results even without directly addressing the personal need. For this to work, it's essential to have adequate self-knowledge. You must really know your own skills and limitations. You have to recognize your need and acknowledge its importance. If you do, some of the 10 workaround tips that follow can prove useful.

   - **People workarounds:**

     (1) Find an internal person to stand in for you when the weakness is in play—a peer, an internal consultant, a friend, or someone from your staff who can assume some of your responsibilities.

     (2) Go outside the organization to find someone to stand in for you when the weakness is in play. This is usually a consultant who specializes in doing what you are not good at.

     (3) Be smart about hiring. Staff your team with people who are good in the areas you are not. Delegate the tasks that bring the weakness into play.

   - **Task workarounds:**

     (4) Trade tasks with a peer. Trade away a task with which you struggle for one in which you excel. This can be a win-win situation in which you get the help you need while providing help to a peer.

(5) Share tasks. Partner with someone to combine tasks and share so that each of you contributes to task elements that play to your individual abilities.

(6) Structure the weakness out. Work with your boss to redesign your job to minimize your weakness. Change your job so that your weakness is no longer so consequential.

- **Change workarounds:**

(7) Change jobs (companies, units, divisions). If you decide that you don't want to work on your needs, do an honest assessment of your strengths and find an organization, a job, or another unit that fits those strengths. If you're not naturally prone to providing customer impact, for instance, you might not belong in a customer service group.

(8) Change careers. Again, if you decide that you don't want to address this need, do an honest assessment of your abilities and motivation and find a different career that is a better fit, a career that suits you. If you are in health care but have a significant weakness in Quality of Work Output (83), as an example, perhaps you should consider a career in which the quality of your work is not so critical.

- **Self-workarounds:**

(9) Declare your weakness. Research shows that admitting weaknesses (within limits) actually increases others' estimations of ability. So, if you start by saying, "As most of you know, I seem to have to work extra hard to meet deadlines," people might be more forgiving.

(10) Redefine yourself. Live with it. If you decide not to address the need, concentrate harder on the things you do well.

Watch Out for Phantom Needs

Sometimes even excellent feedback can identify the wrong need. For instance, even if it's obvious to you and everyone else that you have a problem with Quantity of Output of Work (81), you still need to identify and work on the root cause. You might not be producing acceptable quantity for any number of reasons: you're a perfectionist, you're unorganized, you're unmotivated, you lack proper tools or supplies, you're part of a dysfunctional work team, you lack required technical skills, etc. The key is to identify the improvement remedies that address your true underlying need. If none or only a few of the tips for your identified need seem to make sense to you, check all the cross-references to see if your need is more likely one of these. Then go back to your feedback sources to see if you can discover the true underlying need.

Watch Out for a Weakness Masking an Overused Strength

Sometimes a strength used to extreme turns into a weakness. Each of the 10 Universal Performance Dimensions has a definition of what the skill would look like if overused. You might identify real improvement opportunities by reading the Overuse definitions of your top three strengths to see if what you think is a strength is actually a weakness. If you do have an overused skill, there are competencies identified as compensators that you can work on to balance the overuse. In other words, instead of focusing on dialing back your overused skill (though that might be desirable), you can focus on other skills that will provide balance. Refer to the information that follows to address an overused strength.

Addressing an Overused Strength

Many people get to very responsible positions with a handful of remarkable strengths. Often these people are self-starters, self-reliant, and loners who get things done. They are better managers of projects and ideas than of people. In fact, they often induce stress in others as they set a breakneck pace and drive everyone around them to keep up. They get repeated promotions until they get to a job that's one step beyond the limits of their capabilities.

Others get little feedback and consistently high (often inflated) performance evaluations. Whether promoted or not, they are encouraged to do more of the same, use the strengths that got them where they are. This is fine, of course, until something changes—a new strategy, a change in job responsibilities, or a new leadership direction in the organization. Then, new skills are called for and the current skill portfolio needs an overhaul.

In either case, the person comes to a fork in the road. The path they choose makes a big difference.

One fork is taken by the learning agile. They are open, curious, always looking for ways to continuously improve. When they detect that the assignment is going to require something different—a break from the past, a new direction, a transition—they figure out what's needed. They pursue a number of strategies to develop new ways of thinking and new skills. They also consider workarounds and compensators in order to be successful.

The other fork is taken by a much larger group. When their aims get frustrated, when things are not going the way they are used to, when they are stretched to their limit, they just turn up the volume on the handful of strengths that they already have. Their operating theory is that if a lot is good, more must be even better. If someone can't understand what's being said, just increase the volume. Taken to extreme, they become relentless drivers of themselves and of others. They find it difficult to delegate, to show trust. They take on too much and get frustrated when pure intellectual horsepower can't solve their problems. In this situation, the offenders typically look to place the blame for performance problems on others. Career derailment is just around the corner.

If you find yourself in the second group—if you've received feedback that you do too much of a good thing—here are some general strategies to address the problem.

(a) Crank back on the throttle. That's obvious, isn't it? Stop overdoing it. Do it less. Decrease the volume. As straightforward as that sounds, few can do it and it's the approach least likely to be effective. Here's why. The performer hears suggestions that are counterintuitive. Be less smart. Less results-oriented. Less self-sufficient. Delegate more. Slow down; listen; reflect. Don't be so hard-charging. Do less yourself. Take fewer risks. All this advice runs counter to their experience—they've achieved success exactly because they've been smart, hard-charging, doers. They've been rewarded for that behavior. It's scary, unthinkable really, to do less of the things that have accounted for their success to date. So, even though the suggestion to crank back on the throttle sounds like a no-brainer, it's rarely ever done successfully.

(b) Another strategy is to put a coating on the aspirin to prevent damage to the stomach. Use some other skills you have to lessen the noise and the damage you are causing by the overuse. Keep driving for results but soften the effect by adding listening skills and humor. Keep charging hard but increase communication and feedback. Keep taking risks but keep people better informed. Each of the 10 Performance Dimensions has skills listed after the Overuse definitions that can compensate for the overuse. The compensators decrease the negative effect of the strengths that have gone into overdrive. They decrease the noise and make your strengths more comfortable to others. How many compensators should you use? As many as it takes to get the noise down to a reasonable level.

(c) If you don't have the compensators you need, you're back to the beginning. Use the improvement tips for the compensators to develop them or use the workaround strategies listed above to accomplish a similar result.

Put It All Together

Improvement can utilize all of the strategies presented above. After you know exactly what you need to work on, you can start with a substitute plan that has an immediate effect. Then, midterm, you can use one or more workaround strategies to continue to cover for your lack of skill. While all of this is progressing, you can use the improvement tips in this book to build the skill over the long-term. As you do, be sure to learn from the people you use in your workaround plan. Then, if further improvement is still required, use tasks, special projects, part-time assignments, and even different jobs to finish your development.

A

Appendix B: My Personal Improvement Plan

Section 1 – My Before and After Performance Improvement Picture

Section 2 – Some Causes of Performance

Section 3 – Learnings from "The Map" for Performance Improvement

Section 4 – Performance Improvement and Action Plans

Section 5 – Quotes That Inspire Performance Improvement

Section 6 – Suggested Readings for Performance Improvement

B

Section 1 – My Before and After Performance Improvement Picture

Look to the Unskilled Definitions (from—performance is more like this now) and the Skilled Definitions (to—improve performance to be more like this in the future).

Dimension
Number: _____

From (Unskilled): _____

_____

_____

_____

To (Skilled): _____

_____

_____

_____

Dimension
Number: _____

From (Unskilled): _____

_____

_____

_____

To (Skilled): _____

_____

_____

_____

Dimension
Number: _____

From (Unskilled): _____

_____

_____

_____

To (Skilled): _____

_____

_____

_____

B

Section 1 – My Before and After Performance Improvement Picture

Look to the Unskilled Definitions (from—performance is more like this now) and the Skilled Definitions (to—improve performance to be more like this in the future).

Dimension
Number: _____

From (Unskilled): _____
_____
_____
_____

To (Skilled): _____
_____
_____
_____

Dimension
Number: _____

From (Unskilled): _____
_____
_____
_____

To (Skilled): _____
_____
_____
_____

Dimension
Number: _____

From (Unskilled): _____
_____
_____
_____

To (Skilled): _____
_____
_____
_____

B-3

Section 1 – My Before and After Performance Improvement Picture

Look to the Unskilled Definitions (from—performance is more like this now) and the Skilled Definitions (to—improve performance to be more like this in the future).

Dimension
Number: _____

From (Unskilled): _____
_____
_____
_____

To (Skilled): _____
_____
_____
_____

Dimension
Number: _____

From (Unskilled): _____
_____
_____
_____

To (Skilled): _____
_____
_____
_____

Dimension
Number: _____

From (Unskilled): _____
_____
_____
_____

To (Skilled): _____
_____
_____
_____

Section 1 – My Before and After Performance Improvement Picture

Look to the Unskilled Definitions (from—performance is more like this now) and the Skilled Definitions (to—improve performance to be more like this in the future).

Dimension
Number: _____

From (Unskilled): _____
_____
_____
_____

To (Skilled): _____
_____
_____
_____

Dimension
Number: _____

From (Unskilled): _____
_____
_____
_____

To (Skilled): _____
_____
_____
_____

Dimension
Number: _____

From (Unskilled): _____
_____
_____
_____

To (Skilled): _____
_____
_____
_____

B-5

Section 2 – Some Causes of Performance

(Why is my performance like this? Why do I do things this way?)
Look to "Some Causes" for clues.

Dimension
Number: _____

Comments: _____
_____
_____
_____

Dimension
Number: _____

Comments: _____
_____
_____
_____

Dimension
Number: _____

Comments: _____
_____
_____
_____

Dimension
Number: _____

Comments: _____
_____
_____
_____

Dimension
Number: _____

Comments: _____
_____
_____
_____

Section 2 – Some Causes of Performance

(Why is my performance like this? Why do I do things this way?)
Look to "Some Causes" for clues.

Dimension
Number: _____

Comments: _____
_____
_____
_____

Dimension
Number: _____

Comments: _____
_____
_____
_____

Dimension
Number: _____

Comments: _____
_____
_____
_____

Dimension
Number: _____

Comments: _____
_____
_____
_____

Dimension
Number: _____

Comments: _____
_____
_____
_____

Section 3 – Learnings from "The Map" for Performance Improvement

Dimension
Number: _____

_____

_____

_____

_____

_____

Dimension
Number: _____

_____

_____

_____

_____

_____

Dimension
Number: _____

_____

_____

_____

_____

_____

Dimension
Number: _____

_____

_____

_____

_____

_____

Dimension
Number: _____

_____

_____

_____

_____

_____

Section 3 – Learnings from "The Map" for Performance Improvement

Dimension
Number: _____

_____

_____

_____

_____

_____

Dimension
Number: _____

_____

_____

_____

_____

_____

Dimension
Number: _____

_____

_____

_____

_____

_____

Dimension
Number: _____

_____

_____

_____

_____

_____

Dimension
Number: _____

_____

_____

_____

_____

_____

Section 4 – Performance Improvement and Action Plans

Dimension
Number: _____

Tip #: _____ _____
_____
_____
_____

Plan: _____
_____
_____
_____

Dimension
Number: _____

Tip #: _____ _____
_____
_____
_____

Plan: _____
_____
_____
_____

Dimension
Number: _____

Tip #: _____ _____
_____
_____
_____

Plan: _____
_____
_____
_____
_____

B

Section 4 – Performance Improvement and Action Plans (continued)

Dimension
Number: _____

Tip #: _____ _____
_____
_____
_____

Plan: _____
_____
_____
_____

Dimension
Number: _____

Tip #: _____ _____
_____
_____
_____

Plan: _____
_____
_____
_____

Dimension
Number: _____

Tip #: _____ _____
_____
_____
_____

Plan: _____
_____
_____
_____
_____

B

Section 4 – Performance Improvement and Action Plans (continued)

Dimension
Number: _____

Tip #: _____ _____

_____

_____

_____

Plan: _____

_____

_____

_____

Dimension
Number: _____

Tip #: _____ _____

_____

_____

_____

Plan: _____

_____

_____

_____

Dimension
Number: _____

Tip #: _____ _____

_____

_____

_____

Plan: _____

_____

_____

_____

_____

Section 4 – Performance Improvement and Action Plans (continued)

Dimension
Number: _____

Tip #: _____ _____
_____
_____
_____

Plan: _____
_____
_____
_____

Dimension
Number: _____

Tip #: _____ _____
_____
_____
_____

Plan: _____
_____
_____
_____

Dimension
Number: _____

Tip #: _____ _____
_____
_____
_____

Plan: _____
_____
_____
_____
_____

Section 4 – Performance Improvement and Action Plans (continued)

Dimension
Number: _____

Tip #: _____ _____
_____
_____
_____

Plan: _____
_____
_____
_____

Dimension
Number: _____

Tip #: _____ _____
_____
_____
_____

Plan: _____
_____
_____
_____

Dimension
Number: _____

Tip #: _____ _____
_____
_____
_____

Plan: _____
_____
_____
_____
_____

Section 4 – Performance Improvement and Action Plans (continued)

Dimension
Number: _____

Tip #: _____ _____
_____
_____
_____

Plan: _____
_____
_____
_____

Dimension
Number: _____

Tip #: _____ _____
_____
_____
_____

Plan: _____
_____
_____
_____

Dimension
Number: _____

Tip #: _____ _____
_____
_____
_____

Plan: _____
_____
_____
_____
_____

Section 5 – Quotes That Inspire Performance Improvement

Dimension
Number: _____

Quote: _____
_____
_____
_____

Source: _____

Dimension
Number: _____

Quote: _____
_____
_____

Source: _____

Dimension
Number: _____

Quote: _____
_____
_____

Source: _____

Dimension
Number: _____

Quote: _____
_____
_____

Source: _____

Dimension
Number: _____

Quote: _____
_____
_____

Source: _____

Section 5 – Quotes That Inspire Performance Improvement

Dimension
Number: _____

Quote: _____

_____

_____

_____

Source: _____

Dimension
Number: _____

Quote: _____

_____

_____

Source: _____

Dimension
Number: _____

Quote: _____

_____

_____

Source: _____

Dimension
Number: _____

Quote: _____

_____

_____

Source: _____

Dimension
Number: _____

Quote: _____

_____

_____

Source: _____

Section 6 – Suggested Readings for Performance Improvement

Dimension
Number: _____

Readings: _____
_____
_____
_____

Dimension
Number: _____

Readings: _____
_____
_____
_____

Dimension
Number: _____

Readings: _____
_____
_____
_____

Dimension
Number: _____

Readings: _____
_____
_____
_____

Dimension
Number: _____

Readings: _____
_____
_____
_____

B

Section 6 – Suggested Readings for Performance Improvement

Dimension
Number: _____

Readings: _____
_____
_____
_____

Dimension
Number: _____

Readings: _____
_____
_____
_____

Dimension
Number: _____

Readings: _____
_____
_____
_____

Dimension
Number: _____

Readings: _____
_____
_____
_____

Dimension
Number: _____

Readings: _____
_____
_____
_____

B

B

Appendix C:
Planning and Goal Setting

The research is crystal clear—individuals and teams perform better when they have goals. Not only that, but research shows that when performance goals are set appropriately and communicated clearly, job satisfaction increases, motivation improves, and there is increased acceptance of the performance management process.

The planning and goal-setting phase is focused at the beginning of the performance management cycle. It consists of a series of conversations between the manager and employees that result in a plan of action and a description of the deliverables that will define success for individuals and for the workgroup. The process goes something like this:

- To begin, the manager leads the team in translating the top-level strategic objectives of the organization into goals that are meaningful for the workgroup. This cascading of goals from the top of the organization down through every level provides alignment—it gets everyone on the team pulling in the same direction. If the manager communicates organizational goals clearly, employees will understand how the business intends to succeed and, very importantly, how their specific roles contribute to that success.

- Managers and individuals then draft individual performance goals that align with and support the goals of the workgroup. These draft goals form the basis of an ongoing collaboration between employee and manager.

- Working from the draft performance goals, the manager and employee have one or more working sessions to finalize goals that will serve the employee and work team throughout the business cycle. The working sessions should be two-way conversations that result in understanding and agreement about what will be achieved, how it will be measured, and, at some level, how the work will get done.

- Goals get established, agreed upon, and finalized, but they don't get rigor mortis. They should remain living ingredients in the workplace mix and subject to modification if the needs of the business change. The intent, of course, is that when the goals are established, they will still be as applicable at the end of the business cycle as they were at the beginning. Practically speaking, though, business objectives have a way of evolving. Individual performance goals need to be firm, but malleable enough to shift to serve the business.

Planning and goal setting are perhaps the easiest of all performance management tasks, but they provide a crucial foundation for success of the process.

How to Create a Good Performance Goal

Variations of the SMART acronym are commonly used as an easy-to-remember tool to facilitate performance goal setting:

S—Specific

M—Measurable

A—Attainable, actionable, achievable, aligned, etc.

R—Results-oriented, realistic, etc.

T—Time-bound, time-oriented, etc.

Studies and experience have shown that the best performance goals have the following characteristics:

They are aligned with business strategies. Performance management, above all else, is about aligning performance to achieve a shared purpose. A small team pulling in the same direction will beat a larger team working at cross-purposes every time. The strategic goals of the business can be brilliantly crafted, carefully address each aspect of a balanced scorecard, and have the enthusiastic endorsement of top management. But, in the end, results are achieved by individuals and teams. The most effective goals start at the top of the organization and cascade down through business units, departments, and teams to each individual. At each step down the line, the goals increase in specificity so they can be embraced and owned by that particular level. The result is an array of tailored performance goals reflecting the firm's strategic intent that are distributed throughout the organization and owned by each group and each individual.

There is agreement about what's to be achieved and how it's to be done. Employees should feel a personal sense of ownership and responsibility for their goals. One way to achieve this is through collaborative goal setting. Managers who don't trust employees to help draft goals miss an opportunity. When employees work independently to draft goals, they generally set them higher and have more commitment to achievement than if the manager assigns a goal without employee input. There is still room for manager influence when employees take a lead in goal creation—after the initial draft, managers can collaborate with employees to revise as necessary and ensure all parties are clear on expectations and in agreement.

There is a line of sight that enables employees to see how their achievements impact the organization. It's important for employees to know what needs to be done and by when, but that's not enough. Help them to see the big picture, to have a clear view up and down and across the organization. It's more likely that they will feel responsibility and assume accountability when they know how their performance goals impact other individuals, teams, and business units.

Performance goals and development goals are often related but are different; they should be addressed independently and individualized for the performer. People learn and develop first and foremost from job assignments, so development is certainly considered when crafting and assigning performance goals (see information about using jobs for development in Appendix A). But it's important for managers and employees to be clear, first, about the business objectives to be achieved and then, as a separate issue, consider developmental objectives. Create performance goals that focus specifically on accomplishments that will impact the business. Create distinct development goals to focus on what the employee will learn. Keep these types of goals independent to make it easier to coach employees and to review and appraise their performance as described in Appendices D and E.

Goals are grounded in reality. Performance goals should describe achievements that are within the control of the performer. To the extent possible, the performer should be able to affect the variables that impact the outcome. This will typically vary with the position level of the performer. The higher one goes in an organization, the more accomplishments depend on the work of others and are subject to the unexpected things that happen in the real world. Goals should reflect that reality. To the extent possible, frontline workers should not have goals that are made or broken by the actions of another business unit or the general economy. The CEO, on the other hand, has a role that is expected to foresee problems and create contingency plans. A tanking economy. A natural disaster. Novel tactics from the competition. None of these are in the CEO's control, but the expectations for accomplishment will, nonetheless, be high. The best goals are shaped to fit the role and, as much as possible, rely on performance, not on external factors.

The specifics are nailed down. A performance goal needs to describe what will be achieved with enough precision that, in the end, everyone readily agrees on the outcome. Improve customer service—a worthy goal, to be sure. But it is ambiguous and open to interpretation. What does improved customer service look like? How will it be achieved? Measured? What resources are available to achieve the goal? When is the improvement to be reached? The required level of specificity depends on the maturity, capability, and level of responsibility of the performer. As these elements increase, fewer goal details are generally required. For instance, the vice president of service might have a goal of improving customer satisfaction by 5% as measured by survey results to be administered in the fourth quarter. That's enough specificity to remove ambiguity about the outcome, but information about how the goal is to be accomplished is not defined. She is expected to figure out how to make that happen—how to marshal resources, improve processes, and direct the efforts of the customer service workforce to achieve the goal. A customer service representative, on the other hand, by virtue of his level of responsibility, has less discretion and likely requires more definition in his goals—for example, implement customer service scripts and use the online decision support system during service calls to reduce average call escalation rates to less than 3% in any given week. See the difference? The service rep not only knows what the achievement looks like, he's given specific information about how to achieve the goal.

The results can be readily measured. Put a number to your performance goals. Make them quantifiable. People pay attention to what gets measured. If you can't measure it, you can't evaluate it or manage it. Choose metrics for which measurement methods and processes exist, for which the cost of measurement is not prohibitive, and for which there is shared understanding of the meaning. A goal to improve the effectiveness of supplier relations by 5% as measured by survey in Q3 sounds pretty good on the surface. Let's assume it's aligned with business strategy. It's fairly specific. And, at face value, it's measurable. But, digging deeper, we might find that (a) the survey doesn't yet exist, (b) there's confusion about what supplier effectiveness really means, and (c) even if agreement is reached, the cost exceeds the scope of the budget when all the requirements for creating the survey, administering it, and evaluating survey data are considered.

There is stretch built into performance goals to extend the employee's reach and impact. Generally, people perform best with achievable stretch goals—goals that can realistically be reached by standing tall and putting forth significant effort. Goals set too high or too low demotivate. Goals that are too high are seen as unreasonable and result in employees making token, half-hearted efforts. Goals that are too low let people coast and encourage them to lose focus. This is a balancing act complicated by the need to set stretch goals for individuals as well as business units. Set the bar high, but not completely out of reach.

Results to be achieved are noted clearly in written documentation. Performance goals should first and foremost describe accomplishment rather than activity. Keeping busy, even doing what seems to be the right things, won't much matter if the activity doesn't lead to desired results. Businesses are rewarded for what they deliver. Employees need to understand how they contribute to the deliverables of the business. Goals should reflect those individual contributions and results achieved by the individual. Write goals down in clear, unambiguous language. Make sure the documentation is readily accessible to the performer. Goals are more likely to be completed when they are documented and reviewed periodically.

There are clear time frames and deadlines stated in performance goals. Never underestimate the importance of speed. Speed drives customer satisfaction up and costs down. Speed drives the competition crazy. Deadlines are godsends and are meant to be kept. Putting time bounds on performance goals is the natural way to put an emphasis on speed. Due dates provide focus. They are essential to overcome the natural inclination in many to procrastinate. Without deadlines, the collective goals of the organization become a house of cards that topples as first one goal, then another, is not achieved in a timely manner. Identify the due date as an explicit component of every performance goal.

The 10 Universal Performance Dimensions in Performance Goal Setting

While the following information can stand alone, it is written to reference the *FYI for Performance Management*™ *Companion CD* provided with this book. If you do follow along with the CD, you will gain practice weighting goals and applying Dimensions to goal setting.

Begin by launching the **PM Companion.exe** file on the CD. After reading and acknowledging the terms of use, you will see a screen that displays performance goals for a fictional employee, Terry Truckle.

Here's the scenario: The company CEO has communicated the business goals for the next fiscal year, and the goals have cascaded down through the VP and Director levels. Terry, the Manager of Operations, has considered those business unit goals that are impacted by the Operations function:

- Increase EBIT (earnings before interest and taxes) to 9.5% of sales

- Increase customer satisfaction at least 5% on each customer survey dimension

- Generate 15% of revenue with enhanced or new products

- Increase employee engagement at least 5% as measured by employee survey

- Reduce voluntary turnover by at least 1%

Then, in collaboration with his Director, Terry has created performance goals that are aligned with the company's strategic objectives and recorded them in a Balanced Scorecard format as shown in figure 1 on the following page.

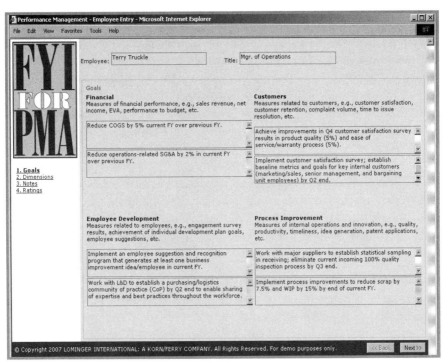

Fig. 1. Goals

The Balanced Scorecard is illustrated here in recognition of the fact that it is used in some form in well over half of large U.S. companies. Robert Kaplan and David Norton introduced the Balanced Scorecard in the early 1990s to help managers take a broader perspective in strategic planning to consider a variety of stakeholders and key measures of success. The Balanced Scorecard can be helpful in the goal-setting process, and it has been linked in some studies to a better connection between strategies and metrics and improved effectiveness in informing employees of strategic intent. While the Balanced Scorecard can be useful when integrated with a performance management process, it is not a prerequisite for creating sound goals or using the 10 Universal Performance Dimensions.

If you examine Terry's goals, you will see that they fit the criteria for well-written goals outlined above. They are aligned with the top-level business objectives. They provide a level of specificity appropriate for the Manager of Operations. They are measurable and time-bound and, though achievable, will require Terry to stretch to achieve them.

After Terry and the Director collaborate to fine-tune the goals, it's time to link the goals to the Performance Dimensions and assign the weight values. From the menu, select **2. Dimensions** to go to the next screen. (In figure 2 below, the Goals and Dimensions are partially displayed. In the *FYI for Performance Management® Companion CD*, the application is fully displayed.)

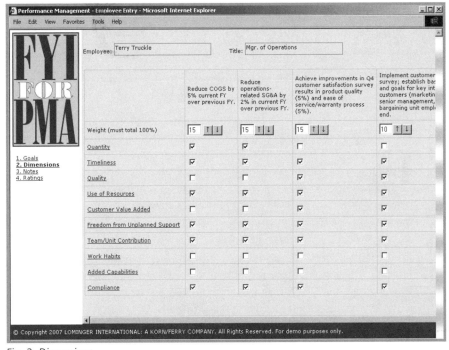

Fig. 2. Dimensions

Weight values can be changed in the Companion CD application but are pre-set with Terry's goals weighted as follows:

- Reduce COGS (cost of goods sold) – 15%

- Reduce SG&A (sales, general, and administrative) expenses – 15%

- Improve customer satisfaction – 15%

- Establish baseline for internal customer satisfaction – 10%

- Implement employee suggestion program – 10%

- Establish CoP (community of practice) – 5%

- Eliminate incoming inspection – 15%

- Reduce scrap and WIP (work in progress) – 15%

The percentages add up to 100% and reflect the Director's view that cost reduction, for instance, is more important than establishing a community of practice. The Companion CD application allows you to change the values, and you would if you were Terry's boss and believed, for instance, that two of your most important strategic business objectives for the year were to increase employee engagement and reduce voluntary turnover. In that case, you would probably choose to give more weight to the goals for the employee suggestion program and CoP, believing that those goals would get employees engaged and lead to better retention. If you weighted those goals more heavily, you would need to reduce the weighting of other goals a like amount.

> The Companion CD application uses the five-point scale which is commonly used in performance management and provides an appropriate amount of differentiation without overcomplicating rating. When implementing performance management, many organizations get hung up on selecting a rating scale and other cosmetic items. Should we use a three-point scale? Four-point? Five-point? Should we use a scorecard? How do we designate the scorecard categories? How many goals in each category? Do we call them goals or objectives? There are many, many design issues that tend to distract managers from what is really important—line managers need to own the process and have meaningful conversations with employees. If meaningful conversations really occur, it doesn't much matter what your forms look like and what kind of rating scale you use.

So, the goals are established. Terry's deliverables are defined. The *what* has been addressed, but not the *how*. For that, the Director needs to decide which of the 10 Dimensions describe *how* the achievements should be accomplished and which of the Dimensions have the greatest impact on achieving the goal. All of the Dimensions may be important for overall performance, but some have a stronger link to specific goals than others. For example, if Terry's goal is to reduce COGS, which of the Dimensions have the strongest relationship to that goal? Terry will need to focus on how much the group produces (81. Quantity of Output of Work), being on time (82. Timeliness of Delivery of Output), the use of available resources (84. Use of Resources), working independently (86. Freedom from Unplanned Support), bringing out the best in the team (87. Team/Unit Contribution), and staying focused (90. Alignment and Compliance). The Performance Dimensions are pre-set in the Companion CD application as follows (these values are also reflected in figure 2 on the previous page):

- Reduce COGS (cost of goods sold)
  81. Quantity of Output of Work

  82. Timeliness of Delivery of Output

  84. Use of Resources

  86. Freedom from Unplanned Support

  87. Team/Unit Contribution

  90. Alignment and Compliance: Walking the Talk

- Reduce SG&A (sales, general, and administrative) expenses
  81. Quantity of Output of Work

  82. Timeliness of Delivery of Output

  84. Use of Resources

  86. Freedom from Unplanned Support

  87. Team/Unit Contribution

  90. Alignment and Compliance: Walking the Talk

- Improve customer satisfaction
  82. Timeliness of Delivery of Output

  83. Quality of Work Output

  84. Use of Resources

  85. Customer Impact/Value Added

  86. Freedom from Unplanned Support

  87. Team/Unit Contribution

  90. Alignment and Compliance: Walking the Talk

- Establish baseline for internal customer satisfaction
  82. Timeliness of Delivery of Output

  83. Quality of Work Output

  84. Use of Resources

  85. Customer Impact/Value Added

  86. Freedom from Unplanned Support

  87. Team/Unit Contribution

  90. Alignment and Compliance: Walking the Talk

- Implement employee suggestion program
  - 82. Timeliness of Delivery of Output
  - 83. Quality of Work Output
  - 84. Use of Resources
  - 85. Customer Impact/Value Added
  - 86. Freedom from Unplanned Support
  - 87. Team/Unit Contribution
  - 90. Alignment and Compliance: Walking the Talk

- Establish CoP (community of practice)
  - 82. Timeliness of Delivery of Output
  - 83. Quality of Work Output
  - 84. Use of Resources
  - 85. Customer Impact/Value Added
  - 86. Freedom from Unplanned Support
  - 87. Team/Unit Contribution
  - 90. Alignment and Compliance: Walking the Talk

- Eliminate incoming inspection
  - 81. Quantity of Output of Work
  - 82. Timeliness of Delivery of Output
  - 83. Quality of Work Output
  - 84. Use of Resources
  - 86. Freedom from Unplanned Support
  - 87. Team/Unit Contribution
  - 90. Alignment and Compliance: Walking the Talk

- Reduce scrap and WIP (work in progress)
  - 81. Quantity of Output of Work
  - 82. Timeliness of Delivery of Output
  - 83. Quality of Work Output
  - 84. Use of Resources
  - 86. Freedom from Unplanned Support
  - 87. Team/Unit Contribution
  - 90. Alignment and Compliance: Walking the Talk

The Director and Terry would have a conversation to discuss why these particular Dimensions are applied. In this scenario, the Director would impress upon Terry the importance of how the work gets accomplished. Discussion points might include:

- Certain Dimensions are important for Terry's role across-the-board. Every goal is linked to Dimensions 82, 84, 86, 87, and 90. Terry is expected to meet every deadline, to use resources wisely in achieving every goal, to not require unplanned support, to support team building in all activities, and to always be a role model that supports the organization's culture.

- Certain Dimensions are not linked to any of Terry's goals. That doesn't mean they're not important. In this case, the Director has elected to not link Terry's goals to Productive Work Habits (88), for instance, because it's not something Terry needs to focus on. The Director knows Terry's work habits are superb, accepts this as a given, and chooses to be selective to provide focus for feedback, coaching, and evaluation in the performance review. This doesn't imply that Terry is only good in these Dimensions. Dimensions are selected to provide focus and criteria for evaluation.

- Some Dimensions are linked to some goals and not to others. Quality of Work Output (83), for instance, is not as applicable in the Director's view to the goals related to cost reduction as it is to the other goals. This doesn't mean quality doesn't apply at all, it just means, again, that the Director has elected to select the Dimensions that Terry should really focus on when working on any particular goal.

After a detailed conversation in which all these things are discussed, Terry will be clear about what needs to be accomplished in the coming year and how the Director expects the work to be conducted. The Dimensions provide focus for Terry. When it's time to make a decision about implementing an internal customer survey, Terry will be certain to consider the quality of the instrument and evaluation process and the value provided by the data for internal customers.

Terry expects to have a series of conversations with the Director throughout the year to review progress toward meeting the goals and to discuss how the job is getting done. We'll see in Appendix D how the Director will use the Dimensions in these conversations to provide feedback and coaching in these sessions. At the end of the year, there shouldn't be any surprises for Terry, since expectations have been clearly communicated and there has been an ongoing dialogue with the Director about what is being achieved and how the work is being done.

C

Feedback and Performance Coaching

Providing feedback and coaching is an ongoing process that spans goal setting and the performance review and impacts both of those bookends of performance management. Feedback is information about behavior that will help an employee know how to change to improve job results. Coaching is assistance provided to help an employee make those changes that lead to job improvement.

Making Feedback Work Better

Nothing good happens until career-minded people get direct, actionable, timely feedback on the things that matter for performance. Critical (corrective) feedback is a must in moving people toward improvement and enhanced job success.

Any feedback intervention should be accompanied with goal setting. There shouldn't be feedback just for its own value. Tied to a job goal or purpose, feedback helps people improve. Tied to nothing, it may backfire. In numerous studies, feedback improved average performance. However, in one-third of the cases, it decreased performance. Why? Because when feedback isn't tied to the tasks at hand, it becomes tied to the only other possibility—the person. Getting better at a particular skill to achieve a goal and perform better can be quite motivating; simply getting better implies that something is wrong with the person. Defensiveness and the need to maintain a positive self-image can quickly get in the way of a productive session.

Any feedback intervention should also include positive and negative data. There is no evidence that accurate negative data hurts people long-term or that positive feedback helps them. The type of data is less important than tying it to criteria of importance. Giving or receiving bad news is no fun, but it is as necessary for performance and growth as detailing strengths. Putting everyone in the same developmental or performance boat against carefully developed criteria takes away a lot of the sting. A fairly run system focuses people where it should—on continuous improvement of job performance.

Coaching More Effectively

There is an orderly process people go through from becoming aware of a need to cementing a new skill into their day-to-day job behavior to getting rewarded for the effort. The process has six steps. Each step requires coaches to apply a different set of skills, use different tools, play different roles, and accomplish different tasks. The six steps must be accomplished in order. You can't skip steps. Employees can and do get blocked at any step and stay blocked for a long time, possibly forever. They can even move backwards to a previous step. Whether it's the manager or another person acting as a coach, the aim is to guide the employee moving through the six steps to improve performance.

For ease of remembering, we call the skill-building process the $A^3B^2C^1$ Growth and Coaching Model, or **A**ll a**B**out **C**oaching. The superscript numbers 3, 2, and 1 refer to the number of steps in each alphabetic sequence.

The six steps of $A^3B^2C^1$ are:

A^3:

1. **Aware**—the coach has to help the employee become aware of the need.
2. **Accept**—the coach has to help the employee accept and take personal responsibility for the need.
3. **Act**—the coach has to help the employee become motivated to do something about the need.

B^2:

4. **Build**—the coach has to help the employee build a plan to improve the skills.
5. **Blend**—the coach has to help the employee blend the new learnings and skills back into the workplace.

C^1:

6. **Consequences**—the coach has to help the organization recognize the employee for the effort and success in addressing the need.

The first goal of coaching is to create a motivated employee with a need—an employee with a need in hand ready to do something about it with no defensiveness and the confidence that something can be done. It involves the first three steps, A^3: The employee becomes aware of the need, takes ownership of it, and becomes motivated to act.

The second goal is having and deploying a development support system that works—a system or process that helps the employee build and execute a plan that works and then supports using those new skills back on the job. It involves the B^2 steps: The employee builds a plan and blends it into the workplace.

Finally, the third goal is activating a recognition and reward system that works—an employee is recognized for the effort and success of addressing the need and then rewarded with hard and soft consequences (pay, promotion, congratulations, more responsibility, etc.). It involves the C^1 step of celebrating accomplishment through positive consequences.

We see the ABC model—three goals and six steps—as the fundamental framework for all coaching, mentoring, 360° facilitation, skill building, and job performance improvement efforts.

A manager, coach, or mentor has six different tasks to do and roles to play. These six phases of coaching have to be accomplished in roughly linear order to work. Each phase builds a foundation for the next stage. Employees will not benefit from a training course on a need (Step 4—Build) they do not accept they have (Step 2—Accept).

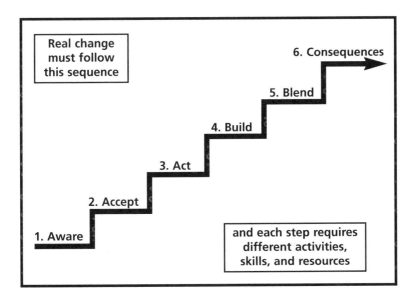

Step 1: Aware—A^1
Help the employee become aware of the need.

Why Step 1?
- No one will or can work on a need of which they are unaware.

- Employees are more right about their strengths and less right about their weaknesses, especially interpersonal weaknesses.

- Self-assessment is the least accurate source when evaluating "soft" weaknesses.

- Most employees need help in understanding themselves.

- Many people are unaware they have a specific need, or any needs for that matter.

Keys to Step 1

- Atmosphere of trust, truth, and honesty

- Credible, understandable feedback from trusted sources

- Drill down to the behaviors

- Use of multi-source, formal feedback (from bosses, peers, direct reports, customers, friends, spouses, etc.) for overwhelming evidence

- Use of multi-method feedback (daily feedback, informal conversations, formal performance reviews, career assessments, and 360°)

- Coach and mentor availability, if needed

- Availability of professional facilitation

- Receptive, non-defensive employee

Coaching Skills Needed for Step 1

- Understanding competencies (needs)

- Diagnosis of needs

- Feedback skills, sometimes very directive

- Convincing and influencing skills

- Proof or evidence skills

Pre–Step 1 Condition: "I am not aware of any critical needs."

Notes and Tips for Step 1 Coaches

Most people don't know themselves well enough to efficiently and effectively improve their current job performance. They need help. If a 35 year-old doesn't yet know his or her weaknesses, he or she needs outside help to discover them.

The first step is simply to help employees realize what others think they need to work on. In many cases, the employee will have a general notion, so the goal is to get behaviorally specific. In other cases, the employee knows some of the issues, so the goal is to help him or her understand the nuances. In some cases, they know one issue but not the others.

The awareness step can be as simple as, "Did you know you don't present well in front of top management." To which the employee replies, "No, I didn't. I thought I was doing OK, but I know that's an important skill so I'll get on it immediately." It can be as difficult as, "That's not true. I'm the best presenter in the organization. They don't know what they're talking about. I'm not interested in hearing anything they have to say about it."

The difficulty of getting through Step 1 depends upon what kind of need is being surfaced. Roughly from easiest to hardest, needs can be classified as follows:

Easiest

1. **Strength.** The task is to help make employees aware that even through they are already good at this, they need to be even better.

2. **Average skills.** The task is to confirm and validate behaviors and skills that are acceptable, just OK, with the goal of improving those behaviors and skills.

3. **Hidden strengths.** The task is to help employees become more confident that others around them think they have skills they are not aware of, with the goal of leveraging the skills and using them more often.

4. **Untested.** The task is to help employees understand that a behavior or skill they have never used before is or will be important. The goal is to test the skill under live fire.

5. **Weaknesses.** Since employees already have a notion they are weak in this area, the task is to add detail and confirming evidence. The goal is for them to see the need in very specific behavioral detail.

6. **Overdone strengths.** The task is to help employees understand a strength done to excess has a dark side. To some extent the current troubles they are having are due less to weaknesses and more to a revved-up strength. The goal is to understand that doing something too much has negative consequences.

7. **Career stallers and stoppers.** The task is to help employees understand that they have one or more of the 19 Career Stallers and Stoppers that frequently derail otherwise promising careers.

8. **Blind spots (THE MOST DIFFICULT).** The task, and this is the hardest, is to help employees understand they have a significant weakness in an area they believe is OK or even strong. This is where the skills of the facilitator and quality of the evidence come into play the most. People can go years and even decades not knowing they have a need in a mission-critical area.

Hardest

Facilitator/Coach Style and Approach in Step 1

Coaching styles range from passive to active, soft to hard, indirect to direct, and aide to expert. We have found that all styles have a chance to be successful, but breakthroughs in Steps 1 (and 2) generally require a more aggressive, direct approach. Remember, you are working with an employee who has 20 to 50 or more years of life experience who doesn't recognize a need. The chances of a soft self-discovery method being successful are slim. In Steps 1 and 2, when dealing with the more difficult types of needs, especially with blind spots, the coach has to be more active, expert, directive, and forceful. Very few break through alone. Otherwise, they wouldn't have blind spots. Steps 3 through 6 can be managed in a more participative, self-discovery manner.

Post–Step 1 Condition: "I can see that others think I have a critical need I should be working on to improve."

Step 2: Accept—A²

Help the employee accept and take ownership of the need.

Why Step 2?

- More people are aware of what others think are their weakness than there are people who accept them as true.

- Taking ownership, becoming a shareholder, and accepting is the first step to real change.

- The need must belong to the employee for any progress to be made.

Keys to Step 2

- Once you have a motivated employee with a need, fixing the problem becomes much, much easier.

- There are a multitude of remedies available, from simple to complex, from quick to long-term, from free to expensive, to help motivated employees with a need to build skills.

- The facilitator needs to assure the employee that progress can be made.

- The facilitator must be able to assure the employee that acknowledging the need is a sign of strength, not of weakness.

- The facilitator must be able to handle the 24 defense scripts employees bring up while trying to get out from under negative feedback.

Coaching Skills for Getting through Step 2

- Conflict management and coolness

- Counseling skills

- Giving good examples

- The rules of evidence and proof-sourcing

Pre–Step 2 Condition: "I know that others think I have a need that ought to be fixed, but I'm not sure it's real."

Notes and Tips for Step 2

Only motivated employees with a need can make progress building competencies and improving performance. A coach should help the employee accept the need. That's where examples and critical incidents come in. Share personal stories about your own needs from the problems you have had to face. Share stories about people you both know who did or did not take ownership of their needs. Talk about the consequences of being defensive or trying to rationalize away the need.

In extreme cases, send the employee to talk to another respected person who is several levels higher in the organization. Have this more senior person reinforce the need and explain why it is critical to rise above it. Also, ask the employee to make self-observations of situations where this need is played out and describe to you the consequences of not being skilled in this area. Until the person says, "This need plays out in ways that are unacceptable for me and my performance," nothing much will happen.

So show some patience. Some people have a hard time acknowledging flaws or admitting that they matter. Many times people never get by this second step. They are forever blocked at knowing others think they have a need but denying it is true.

We have been collecting defense scripts that people use when defending themselves against negative feedback. In the past 20+ years, we have facilitated thousands of feedback sessions. All the following are real things people have said (and continue to say) in the face of negative information coming from multi-source assessments:

1. My raters really don't know me that well (and therefore the feedback is not true).

2. The wrong people evaluated me (and therefore the feedback might be true, but isn't important).

3. My job makes me act this way; I'm not really like this (and therefore the feedback is about a condition and not really about me).

4. Some of my raters have it in for me (and therefore they falsified their feedback to hurt me).

5. The computer must have scored this wrong.

6. My raters don't understand the situation I'm in.

7. All my strengths are all right, but my weaknesses aren't.

8. The norms don't really apply to me.

9. I used to be this way, but I've since changed.

10. Nobody really understands me.

11. This must be someone else's report.

12. My boss doesn't like me and marked me low because of it.

13. My raters didn't understand the questions.

14. My raters don't speak English very well.

15. This was a bad time to do this assessment.

16. I actually filled out all the surveys myself, but apparently I did it incorrectly.

17. This can't be my report because I'm perfect.

18. I wasn't like this in my last job.

19. My boss asked me to be this way; actually, I'm quite different.

20. My raters are just jealous of my success.

21. I purposely picked raters who don't like me.

22. It's all accurate; I just don't care.

23. I've changed since the assessment was completed.

24. This is just what I expected, but it's not me.

Coaching for Step 2 Acceptance

- Typical reactions to feedback: Up to one-third are deniers, devastated, or hostile; one-third are basically OK—they know they have the need but aren't really motivated to do much; and one-third are energized by finally figuring out what it was that wasn't working for them and how to fix it. One-half of these are usually good performers who want to get better, and the other half are people scared they will not get the next promotion or will be fired.

- For the true deniers, ask them to consider why they might make the same statement about someone else. Get a commitment that they will have a discussion about the need with someone who has their best interests at heart. Recite your view (and that of others) and what people mean by saying it. Ask what the consequences are of people believing it.

- If someone is really down, say, "People don't keep doing things that don't pay off. How has doing that worked for you in the past?" Explain how strengths left ungoverned sometimes tip over to weaknesses. Turn the negative energy into a positive by getting the employee to see his or her downsides as consequences of strengths.

- When employees are hostile, let them talk. Reflect calmness back to them. Then, take whatever is said and restate it in an exaggerated way. "So, there's absolutely no truth to this evaluation." "So this is totally unfair." Often this will get the employee to acknowledge the issue.

- Go after the toughest issue first unless the employee is really hurting. Pick what he or she is mostly likely to remember.

- When an employee is clearly poor at something like team building or strategy, ask, "What's getting in the way?" Find out what the person doesn't like to do and how he or she understands the issue. You will generally find the person has a poor understanding and needs a fresh mental map before much progress can be made. For example, poor team builders usually not only lack skill, they lack attitude, may not see the value of teams, don't think like team builders think, and aren't tuned in to reading and learning from other people.

- Have the employee describe tough situations that are stumbling blocks. "Take me inside a meeting where that happened. What did you say? When did you first notice…?" What triggers you? What are your hot buttons?" Work with the employee to identify what is getting in the way and what hits hot buttons. Have him or her focus on triggers that lead to loss of control or frustration and devise simple countermeasures for those triggers.

- The essence of acceptance is when the employee can vividly describe consequences that are personally unacceptable and is able to take the coach inside situations to describe poor behaviors and the undesirable consequences.

Facilitator/Coach Style and Approach in Step 2

This is the most difficult and critical step. If you can't pull a learner through Step 2, you are dead in the water. Remember, you are working with an employee who has 20 to 50 or more years of life experience who doesn't accept a documented need. Again, as in Step 1, the chances of a soft self-discovery method being successful are slim. In Step 2, when dealing with the more difficult types of needs, especially with blind spots, the coach has to be more active, expert, directive, and forceful. Very few break through to acceptance alone. The 24 defense mechanisms are in full force. Otherwise, they wouldn't have blind spots. Steps 3 through 6 can be managed in a more participative, self-discovery manner.

Nothing happens until the learner owns the need.

Post–Step 2 Condition: "I have a need."

Step 3: Act—A³

Help the employee to see the value in working on the need.

Why Step 3?

- More people accept that they have weaknesses or needs than there are people who commit to taking action to fix the problem.

- Nothing happens until the employee wants something to happen.

- Motivation to work on the problem is the elixir for real change.

Keys to Step 3

- Success profiles that illustrate why this need is important

- Proof stories that describe what has happened to others with this need

- Consequence management that defines what will happen if the need is not addressed and, alternatively, what will happen if there is success

- Modeling the skill

- Creditably demonstrating that the need can be successfully addressed and telling stories about others doing so

- Mentoring

- Atmosphere of optimism and hope

Coaching Skills for Step 3

- Influencing

- Proof skills

- Success storytelling (implying you would have to know some)

- Negotiating

- Visioning what would happen if the person improves at something

- Relating history of people who did and did not do something about this need

Pre-Step 3 Condition: "I have a need but I'm not sure I want to do anything about it. I wonder if it's worth it to work on this need."

Notes and Tips for Step 3

As we did above for Acceptance, we have been collecting reasons why people who admit and accept (Step 2) they have a need still don't think they should work on it. Again, all real.

1. No one above me is good at this (and therefore why should I work on this?).

2. I've done well enough thus far without it (and therefore I can make it all the way with this need unaddressed).

3. I don't think I could really change enough to make a difference.

4. I don't think this is a real requirement for success around here.

5. This would be too hard to do.

6. This would take too long to do me any good.

7. "They" (the organization, top management, my bosses) don't support fixing this here.

8. I don't understand why this is important to me.

9. I am what I am; they just need to accept me for what I am.

10. I like the way I am.

11. It's too late for me to change.

12. I've decided to leave, so this is no longer important.

13. Even if I fixed this, it really wouldn't help me that much.

14. Fixing this will make me less effective.

15. Fixing this is not worth the effort.

16. I'm not ready to fix this yet; I'm too busy.

17. I just got done fixing something else; now you want me to fix this, too.

18. No one else around me is working on fixing this or anything else.

19. I've never seen anyone like me change this.

20. I don't see the payoff for me to go through the effort to fix this.

The task in Step 3 is to convince employees that the need they admit to is important enough to work on. The time to act is now.

What the facilitator must do is find out what drives the employee, what gets the person out of bed in the morning. Legacy? Promotion? Job satisfaction? Pleasing others? Power? Being liked? Being respected? Somewhere in the person's motivation hierarchy is the key to moving from knowing and admitting to acting.

This is usually accomplished by a series of positive or negative what-ifs. What if you were better at presenting? What if you were better at listening? What if you were an above-average strategist? What would that do for you? What would it lead to? Is there a payoff for you somewhere in there?

The more drastic process is a series of negative consequence what-ifs. What if you don't learn to be a better strategist? What if you don't learn to work more smoothly with direct reports? What has happened to others you or we know who didn't get better in these areas? Are you willing to live with the possible consequences of never fixing this?

Remember, nothing happens until the employee wants something to happen.

The task is to move from knowing (A^1) to acceptance (A^2) to commitment to act (A^3).

Post–Step 3 Condition: "I have a need I want to work on."

Step 4: Build—B^1

Help the employee create a plan to build the skill.

Why Step 4?

- Once you have a motivated employee with a need, fixing the problem and building the skills become much easier.

- But most people don't know how skills and careers are built. They have had this need for years and have not done anything much to fix it.

- There are a multitude of remedies available, from simple to complex, from quick to long-term, from free to expensive, to help people build skills.

Keys to Step 4

- Effective improvement support system

- Efficient use of improvement resources

- Multifaceted approach

- Safe-haven practice

- In-process/in-progress feedback

- Action learning

- Atmosphere of support

Coaching Skills for Step 4

- Knowledge of skill-building technology

- Knowledge of the Broadband system

- Access to resources

- Willingness to commit and execute resources

- Teacher/coach/role model

Pre-Step 4 Condition: "I have a need to work on and I want to work on it, but I don't know how. I need help building a plan that will work for me."

Notes and Tips for Step 4

When you have motivated employees with a need, they usually want to launch into fixing the need in a hurry. Yes, even after 10 years of not doing anything.

Look first at the Personal Job Improvement Plan in Appendix A that lists ways to develop in any area and pick any that fit for the employee. In addition to development, there are substitutes and four workaround strategies to address a need. This improvement plan can be used as a basic core for any coaching session. For more details on these methods, please see *Broadband Talent Management: Paths to Improvement.*

Traditionally, development has focused on "fixing the weakness." It meant building a new skill. It meant improving the ability to do something. It called for being better at something. While that is still true, there are other viable options. The venerable IDP—Individual Development Plan, or the PDP—Personal Development Plan still reigns. But now, it comes in three flavors:

The Classic—Moving a weakness to OK or average or out of the noise zone.

The OK to Good—Moving an average skill to above average.

The Good to Great—Moving an above-average skill to outstanding or exceptional.

The implied objective of the usual IDP or PDP is to move a weakness to a strength. That is a big and unlikely goal. Few people ever achieve that. It seems more likely that a person would move through these three kinds of plans sequentially. If you achieve the first, then move to the second.

In addition to working directly on the need, there are two other kinds of plans that successfully "address the need."

The first is a Workaround Plan. In a workaround plan, the person gets the task done that is being hampered or blocked by the need in another way. There are at least 10 other ways to neutralize a weakness or cover for a need. Those 10 ways are listed in Appendix A. The simplest workaround is to get someone else to do it. In exchange, you do something for that person in an area where you are better skilled than he or she is.

The second is a Substitute Plan. In a substitute plan, the person uses something else they are already good at to substitute (act in place of, accomplish the same thing as) for the missing skill. Every competency or skill can be covered by other competencies and skills. For example, the appropriate use of humor can help manage conflict. The substitute codes for all of the Dimensions are listed in Appendix F.

For the IDP or PDP plans, look through and select remedies mapped to the Dimensions that apply. Lay out a plan and a schedule with the employee. The action plan should include at least three items to be worked on immediately and refreshed every time one task gets completed. Agree on measures to track when actions are taken and when improvements have been made. Set a specific time frame of no more than one month for focused actions to occur. If the time frame is longer than one month (or indefinite), it's unlikely that much will occur.

In selecting specific steps, consider:

- The energy of the employee
- How much time is available for development and improvement actions
- How practical each selected step is in the context and culture of the organization
- Strategies for starting small and building up as improvements are made
- How to build in some early successes

Help the employee with resources. Development and job improvement take time and money. The employee needs access to tasks, projects, and assignments. The need may call for expensive courses or time off for parallel tasks (such as working on community projects). You can help by running interference in the organization and arranging for the employee to work with others in the organization who can be helpful.

The employee will need continuous feedback, emotional support, and reinforcement. When developing any skill, most actually get worse before they get better. It can be a real emotional struggle. In order to work on any need with a big gap, the person has to let go of one trapeze—the past—and grab for the other trapeze—the future—before any progress is possible. In between the two trapezes is nothing but air with no safety net. Many never let go of the first trapeze. You have to help the person realize that forgetting past habits is just as important as learning new ones.

Many times all that's necessary is that you listen and provide a friendly sounding board, but don't make yourself the sole source of feedback or comfort. Remedies work best in multiples. Encourage the employee to get the maximum number of perspectives, not just yours.

People who have made a negative appraisal of the employee's skills will be slow to recognize incremental differences. The employee may get demoralized when others don't recognize early progress. You may have to chart and mark off progress on the BARS (see Appendix G for BARS ratings) to keep spirits up. Have the employee get feedback from people who aren't so familiar and don't have strongly formed negative opinions.

Post–Step 4 Condition: "I have a plan that will fix the problem and I am happily working on it and I am making progress."

Step 5: Blend—B²

Help the employee integrate the new skills back into the workplace.

Why Step 5?

- Many change efforts fail because integrating the new skills back into the workplace is not planned or supported.

- Support must extend beyond the fix for the effort to work.

- The job is not done until the job is done right.

- Bosses and coworkers prefer that people stay the same and sometimes resist accepting new and changed behaviors.

Keys to Step 5

- Support from the boss and coworkers in the workplace

- Educated boss/mentor and coworkers

- No-fault practice

- In-process/in-progress feedback

- Confirming feedback

- Atmosphere of finishing the job

Coaching Skills for Step 5

- Understanding the blending process

- Patience

- Affirmation

- Team coaching

- Working behind the scenes

- Influence in the workplace

Pre–Step 5 Condition: "I have learned some new skills and behaviors and addressed the need successfully. Now I need a plan to integrate the new behaviors back into the workplace."

Notes and Tips for Step 5

Many employees get to the point where they have learned some new skills and behaviors only to have them chilled when they try to apply them to the terminally busy and insensitive workplace. Say the need is to talk less and listen more, a common first step for those seen as arrogant. The employee volunteers for a task force assignment featuring an unfamiliar segment of the business. From this, new skills are learned—how to listen between the lines and ask questions to pick the brains of the more knowledgeable members. The employee learns how to best contribute and impresses others with a willingness to work, not just to learn. But back with the regular workgroup, no one notices any change. When the employee listens and asks questions, gives others the benefit of the doubt, and tries to appreciate other perspectives, no one seems to notice or they assume the interest is insincere. They suspect the employee is trying a new tactic driven by a personal agenda. Some even ask if the employee feels all right because they don't see the previous aggressive, impatient behavior.

What is actually happening is that the employee has changed, and it can take up to eight positive instances of a new behavior before people begin to alter their views and question the previous negative behavior. This is the critical blending point. The boss has to be an active party in helping the employee blend back into the work environment with new behaviors and skills. The solution might be to have the employee meet with coworkers to explain the needs, attempts to fix the problem, and what is needed in support of the new behaviors. In the meeting, the employee should explain what will be done differently to support the work team. Research indicates this is usually the best way to turn around a negative situation. The employee admits the need, asks for help, and provides help. Then people are more prepared to give the benefit of the doubt. They know how tough it is to change.

Post–Step 5 Condition: "I have integrated the new skills and behaviors I have learned into my daily portfolio of skills."

Step 6: Consequences—C[1]
Help the organization respond to the successful effort the person has gone through by delivering the promised rewards and consequences.

Why Step 6?
- The successful development and performance improvement effort must be properly and fairly rewarded for any future attempts to be effective on the part of this individual and indirectly for anyone else.
- Promised or implied consequences have to come true.

Keys to Step 6
- Workplace response to changes

- Staffing/succession actions

- Pay change

Coaching Skills for Step 6

- Assurance that effort leads to reward

- Influence on the reward system

- Helping the organization deliver on promises

- Managing the reward system

Pre-Step 6 Condition: "*I have worked hard and successfully learned and integrated new skills and behaviors into my portfolio; I now want the promised reward.*"

Notes and Tips for Step 6

Many times the proposition for change is the following two scripts:

1. If you don't change (build this skill, address this need, adopt this new behavior), the following bad things will happen:

    - You won't get promoted.

    - You won't get a choice assignment.

    - You may get terminated.

    - You may not have the impact you desire.

2. If you do change (build this skill, address this need, adopt this new behavior), the following good things will happen:

    - You will get the promotion you've been waiting for.

    - You will get the pay raise you've been waiting for.

    - You will get back on your career track.

    - You can keep your job.

    - You will be included as a real member of the team.

    What is at stake is the credibility of the development or improvement process for:

    - This one employee. Will the person ever work on anything again?

    - All employees in the organization. Will anyone work on anything?

If the predicted consequences do not occur, this employee will probably not work on any other needs. If this happens frequently, others in the organization will come to believe that this development stuff is a sham and that there is no real payoff for going through the painful process of exploring and working on needs.

It's up to all the combined coaches, mentors, bosses, HR, and top management to assure that the projected good and bad consequences happen. If they don't regularly, then no development or performance improvement process or system will do anyone any good.

Some possible rewards include:

- Recognition by the boss
- Recognition by coworkers
- A team celebration
- A roast, applauding changes by parodying past behavior
- Merit pay or bonuses
- A special assignment as a developmental project
- Being placed in the queue for more challenging jobs
- Increase in base pay

You may be the only person who really knows what the employee has gone through. Find ways for the employee to demonstrate newly developed skills and behaviors. Take the measurements and milestones the two of you have established seriously. When one is met or exceeded, celebrate it!

Post-Step 6 Condition: "I have been fairly rewarded for my efforts, and I am willing to get to work on my next need."

Summary of the ABC Process

Goal 1: Creating a Motivated Employee with a Mission-Critical Need

A^1	From:	I don't have a need.
	To:	Others think I have a need.

A^2	From:	Others think I have a need.
	To:	I have a need.

A^3	From:	I have a need, but I have no interest in working on it.
	To:	I want to work on this need.

Goal 2: Having and Deploying Resources to Help the Employee Address the Need

B⁴

From: I want to work on this need, but I don't know how.

To: I have a plan to work on this need and it's working.

B⁵

From: I have learned new and different behaviors, but I'm having trouble implementing them.

To: I am now working and behaving differently and it's successful.

Goal 3: Delivering the Promised or Implied Rewards and Consequences

C⁶

From: I have successfully addressed the plan, but I have not been rewarded.

To: I have received the reward and the consequences I was promised, and I am ready for more.

More General Coaching Tips

If you are the coach:

- Being an expert is a matter of theme and pattern recognition and applying insights from that recognition. It's not just giving answers. What are you an expert in? What keys do you look at? How can you pass those on?

- Always explain your thinking. The role of a coach is to teach someone how to think/act in new ways. Giving the person solutions won't help unless he or she knows why and how you came up with them.

- Before you give advice, ask yourself why this is a strength for you or others you know. What are the first items you would teach as keys to help the person form umbrellas for understanding? How did you learn to do this? What were your key experiences? Who helped you? Use these insights and the Skilled definition of the Dimensions to write a list of key behaviors that the person can use as targets.

If you are the person being coached:

- Remember that it is the coach's role to help you grow. Your coach may be an expert in the developmental or improvement process and/or an expert in your need area. You will gain most if you focus less on the coach's solutions and more on why and how the coach arrived at the solution. Ask the coach to explain—many won't do this unless asked.

- How does your coach teach? What adjustments does the coach make for you? Ask for feedback on how you're doing.

- Set projects for yourself that give you feedback on how well you are gaining expertise in an area. If you are working on active listening, set five specific situations in which you actively listen. With your coach, set results in advance that will be evidence of your effectiveness.

- In the case of a boss/mentor as a coach, distance your feelings from the relationship and try to study things that work for this person. Focus on what the person does well.

- More effective learners reduce insights to rules of thumb. If your coach is an expert, what five things does the coach do that you think you could do? What five rules of thumb are you learning from your own efforts? If you have a developmental coach, what have you learned about how to learn and develop that you could use again?

- Unresolved defensiveness will kill any coaching effort. Resolve to accept whatever you are told and at least consider giving it a try. After all, you're the one with the need.

Reviewing Development

The guidelines above are, for the most part, equally appropriate for discussions with employees about improving job performance and about personal and career development. We suggest you separate performance improvement conversations from career development discussions. It's hard enough for managers to be direct and focus on performance issues without having an escape hatch to easily divert the conversation to development and career path. Performance management discussions should focus on the job, on goal accomplishment, on work behaviors, and on ways to improve performance. Set aside other times that are dedicated for discussion of learning plans, development, and career advancement.

If you're separating job improvement discussions from development discussions, it follows then that 360° feedback should be limited to development. This is firmly supported by the research that overwhelmingly indicates 360° feedback is best limited to development and not tied to performance reviews, promotions, or compensation.

Using the 10 Universal Performance Dimensions in Coaching

While the following information can stand alone, it is written to reference the *FYI for Performance Management Companion CD* provided with this book. If you do follow along with the CD, you will gain practice applying Dimensions to feedback and coaching.

Begin by launching the **PM Companion.exe** file on the CD. After reading and acknowledging the terms of use, you will see a screen that displays performance goals for a fictional employee, Terry Truckle. From the menu, select **3. Notes**.

Continuing the scenario from Appendix C, it's midyear and there is an ongoing conversation between Terry and the Director related to Terry's performance. Most of the conversations are informal and focus on one or two issues at a time. The Director has also scheduled quarterly conversations that are more formal and allow for feedback and coaching on all of Terry's goals. As the year progresses, the Director captures critical incidents to share with Terry and, during the more formal conversations, documents feedback and coaching suggestions in the Notes as shown in figure 3.

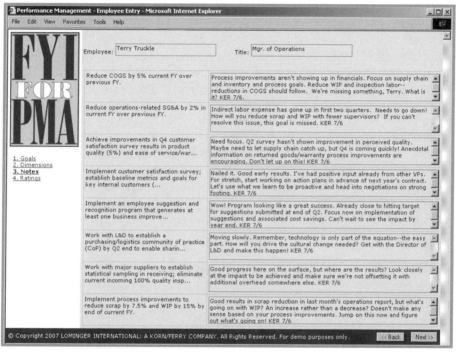

Fig. 3 Notes

Let's see how the Director might use the coaching model and the BARS associated with the Dimension to get Terry to "move the needle" on performance related to a goal previously defined and agreed upon (see Appendix C): to establish a purchasing/logistics community of practice (CoP) to facilitate knowledge sharing in the organization.

The Director is not satisfied with progress to date. Although Terry has succeeded in establishing a technology infrastructure to support a CoP, employees in general aren't using the system, and the Director believes the problem is that Terry has not attended to the cultural change required for this initiative to be successful. Terry is a hard driver and has pushed a solution through but has not worked closely with the Director of Learning and Development and other key change agents in the organization to effectively manage change.

In conversation, the Director begins to raise Terry's awareness of the need by asking questions about usage of the system. Digging deeper, the Director asks Terry about root causes that are hindering the adoption of this initiative and about Terry's lack of expertise in change management. The Director asks how things might be different if Terry had worked more closely with others in the organization.

The Director wants to coach Terry on the overused strength in Dimension 86—Freedom from Unplanned Support. Referring to Appendix G, the Director can help Terry understand how overuse could be a contributor to the problem. The Rating 10 description includes this wording: "Is so driven to work independently that they are unreasonable loners. Doesn't want any help, goes own way and works on own objectives. May waste time and resources working on the wrong things or in the wrong way." The Director points out that a rating of 9 (Exceeds +) is the target, and Terry can best achieve that by looking to other behaviors to strengthen.

Further, the Director points Terry to Dimension 87—Team/Unit Contribution, and uses the BARS Rating 4 (Meets −) to help paint the picture of Terry's current level of performance. The rating reads: "Is a little less helpful than average to the rest of the team or other units in getting their work done or in cooperating with them. Sometimes resists sharing resources and information or taking time when they're busy." The Director asks Terry how the needle might be moved to improve performance in this Dimension.

As Terry listens to the Director and answers the questions, light begins to dawn, and with it comes acknowledgement that the CoP is not working as intended and why. With awareness, acceptance, and a willingness to act, Terry is more than halfway toward addressing the need.

The Director encourages Terry to improve in two areas to compensate for the overused strength. Peer Relationships and Building Effective Teams are two of the compensators listed for Dimension 86 that fit Terry's need. There are remedies provided for Dimension 87 and related to both competencies, as well. The Director helps Terry build an improvement plan that includes working on influencing skills (peer relationships) and establishing a common cause and shared mind-set (team building).

In the process of creating the plan, the Director guides Terry, without being directive, but commitment is made to help Terry with blending the improvement activities; the Director will give a nudge to Terry's peers to get them moving in the right direction, too. The Director talks about the consequences for achieving the goal as well as consequences for failing to meet the goal.

D

APPENDIX E: PERFORMANCE REVIEWS

The quality of performance reviews is driven by two factors. The first involves preparation and application of best practices for the performance review process. The second is more subjective and variable. The second is about courage—managerial courage—the courage of the boss to deliver timely, honest, and sometimes critical and corrective feedback. The second factor is by far more critical to successful reviews. Looking at it in chart form:

	Lower Courage	Higher Courage
More Preparation	3	1
Less Preparation	4	2

The best of all worlds is Cell 1—good preparation and high courage. The boss is well prepared with good news and bad and has no trouble delivering either. Next best is probably Cell 2—less preparation but higher courage. Perhaps the boss hasn't done all of the homework needed, but the discussion is rich and direct. Not everything gets covered, but enough gets talked about to move the needle. Next best is Cell 3—here, the boss has done a good job getting prepared but holds back, especially on the critical feedback. In many of those cases, the key topics are covered in the paperwork but not highlighted in the discussion. Worst case is Cell 4—inadequate preparation and unwillingness to deliver a tough-love conversation.

Research has documented the managerial courage issue. Many managers, whether they are prepared or not, have trouble delivering critical feedback. In our research, managerial courage is in the bottom-five rated skills out of 67 for managers and executives by the people who receive feedback from them.

This book doesn't address the courage issue. We have other products and solutions for that issue. This book and this appendix address best practices for preparation.

The performance review is a key element of performance management and a key enabler of individual and organizational effectiveness. When performance reviews are poorly executed, the downside can be significant and range from a loss of productivity, talent, and morale problems to unpredictable negative behavior.

For organizations that do the entire process and reviews well, the outcomes can be significant:

- **There aren't many surprises.** The daily dialogue between manager and employee has provided ample information, explicit feedback, and helpful coaching along the way, so the performance review might seem anti-climactic. Although typically more comprehensive and protracted in one sense, in another, the performance review is just one more dialogue in a string of conversations that have been occurring throughout the year.

- **The focus is on observable, measurable accomplishments and behaviors.** Subjectivity and emotions are minimized.

- **The tone is forthright and positive.** Bad news and critical remarks—as well as good news and praise—are delivered constructively, honestly, and in the spirit of helping the organization and the employee.

- **There is differentiation.** Top performers, solid performers, marginal performers, and under-performers are all accurately identified.

- **People perform better.** Employees receive direction, support, and encouragement to grow, develop, and perform to the best of their abilities. Year over year their value to the organization grows as they provide meaningful accomplishments that support the organization's strategic objectives. In doing so, their jobs are enriched, and they become increasingly engaged in the business.

- **The organization improves.** A high-performance culture is nourished. Top performers thrive and benefit from differentiated rewards and development. Marginal improvers get better or are moved out of the organization to make room for stronger contributors. Top performance becomes the expectation, the norm.

- **There is a clear link to rewards.** Rewards are used to reinforce the high-performance culture. Differentiation in compensation is consistent with the differentiation in performance.

Be Prepared

Prepare adequately for the review. Assemble all relevant information, including:

- Documentation of goals

- Dimensions linked to the goals

- Manager's informal file containing notes compiled from feedback and coaching sessions and anything else pertaining to working with the individual

- Formal reports, status checks, and metrics around goals

- The employee's job improvement and/or development plan

- Anything else pertinent to the review

Assign ratings for each of the applicable Performance Dimensions in advance of the review. Record notes, especially critical incidents, which illustrate the lower rating you've selected on each behaviorally anchored rating scale (BARS—see Appendix G). Consider the performance, the accomplishments, of the employee related to each goal. Use your organization's rating scale to rate the performance of each goal and also determine an overall rating that represents a composite of achievement on all goals. More information on rating performance is provided in this appendix.

Have an Effective Conversation

As outlined in Appendix D, here are some guidelines that will help any conversation about performance to be more productive:

- Create a clear agenda that outlines the objectives of the review session. Share it in advance with the employee to set expectations.

- Consider time and space. Clear your schedule to allow plenty of time for a productive conversation. Meet in a private, neutral location that is free from distractions. Turn off your cell phone and focus on the employee. Don't rush.

- Be direct. Get to the important points early. Follow a script to make sure you don't miss important points. Don't rely on your memory. Review goal achievement, behaviors for each selected Dimension, and where the behavior falls on the associated BARS.

- Be specific and describe critical incidents to illustrate the appropriateness of the selected ratings.

- Don't sandwich criticism between praise. Recognize accomplishments and address areas of concern and needs for improvement distinctly.

- Actively listen. Probe for understanding. Don't assume silence implies agreement.

- Stay in control of the conversation. Acknowledge emotions but don't get emotional. Avoid defensive postures and body language. Relax.

- Discuss the impact of performance on others and the organization. Provide specific examples to illustrate the linkage between individual behaviors and accomplishments and resulting outcomes for the team, business unit, and organization.

- Ask for ideas and input. Ask questions. What worked well? Not so well? How could results have been improved? What kind of support do you need going forward? Remember, it's a conversation, not a lecture.

- Agree on next steps. Don't leave the review without an action plan for the employee and the manager. Include specifics on how and when there will be follow-up.

- Listen to the employee's views about performance ratings. Allow the employee to record his or her views whether or not in agreement.

- Summarize. Ask for acknowledgement of all the points covered.

- Express appreciation for the employee's contribution and active participation in the review process.

Viewing Accomplishments and Dimensions

While the following information can stand alone, it is written to reference the *FYI for Performance Management Companion CD* provided with this book. If you do follow along with the CD, you will gain practice applying Dimensions to the performance review process.

Begin by launching the **PM Companion.exe** file on the CD. After reading and acknowledging the terms of use, you will see a screen that displays performance goals for a fictional employee, Terry Truckle. From the menu, select **4. Ratings**.

Continuing the scenario from Appendices C and D, it is now time for Terry's review. The screen is pre-set to reflect the Director's ratings for Terry as displayed in the screen shown in figure 4. You'll see that each of Terry's eight goals have been rated as having met, partially met, or exceeded expectations. Also, a value has been assigned for each of the Dimensions selected (based on the BARS rating scale—see Appendix G).

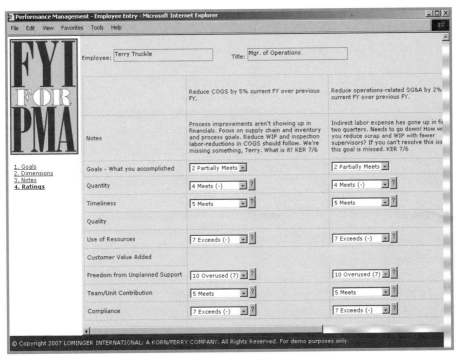

Fig. 4. Ratings

While the values are pre-set in the Companion CD application, you can make changes in the values on the Ratings screen and see it reflected in the averages on the Performance Review Summary report.

This rating process opens up several approaches for the Director to work with Terry in the performance review discussion. Both goal accomplishment and behaviors

(Dimensions) can and should be addressed, but depending on circumstances and individual needs, the focus may change.

Focus on Goal Achievement *(What)*: For instance, the Director might choose to concentrate the discussion on goal achievement and discuss in detail how well Terry's outcomes matched the results targeted by each goal. The discussion would center on the values in the second row of the matrix that reflects the goal ratings. This approach can be especially effective when the work environment is fairly stabile and the employee has lots of control over how goals are achieved. Even in this case, though, the Director will dive down into the Dimensions to look at how the work was done to provide a better understanding of why particular results were achieved and to provide coaching for job improvement. For instance, Terry failed to meet the first two goals which were related to cost reduction. The Director gave Terry a rating of 10 (overuse) on Dimension 86, Freedom from Unplanned Support, as related to these goals. Note that an overuse rating translates into a value of 7 (see Appendix G). The related discussion might focus on how Terry's ability to work independently was overdone when attempting to reduce costs. In the Director's view, if Terry had sought support from the finance group rather than going it alone, the goals would have likely been achieved.

Focus on Dimensions *(How)*: An alternative approach is for the Director to focus on Dimension ratings. This might be the most useful approach when goals have been in flux and changed frequently during the period covered by the review or when factors outside the employee's control impacted goal achievement. Of course, accomplishments would still be discussed, but the focus in this case would be on behaviors. For instance, the Director might choose to concentrate on Dimension 87, Team/Unit Contribution. Terry's average rating on this Dimension is 5.75, which is just average or slightly above average, but the Director's expectation for a Manager of Operations is much higher. The intention here is to get Terry to move the needle up in this area.

There are tremendous advantages of rating performance by considering both goal achievement and behaviors:

- Well-written goals that are specific and measurable and the use of behaviorally anchored rating scales (BARS) remove most subjectivity. Ratings are more readily accepted by employees. There is much more detail and defensibility in the ratings.

- Rating goals provides a focus on accomplishments that impact business results. The employee gets a better understanding of business needs, mission, and strategy.

- Rating behaviors gives the employee more concrete, actionable performance aspects to work on. Coaching is easier and becomes more effective.

- The process promotes differentiation of performers. There is adequate gradation in the Dimension scales to discriminate between individuals in a workgroup, even if they all achieve roughly the same results.

If you select the **Next** button, you will see a summary report that presents the average rating Terry received on each of the Dimensions and also for Goal Achievement.

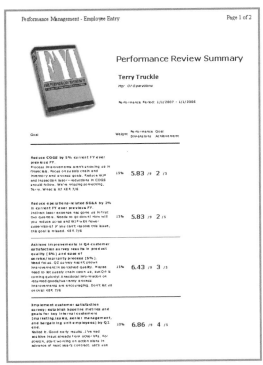

Fig. 5. Performance Review Summary

Rating Errors

Rating precision and objectivity will be greatly enhanced if goals are well written and the descriptions provided in the BARS are carefully considered and compared to performance. Still, managers are human and prone to subjectivity and rating errors. Most rating errors can be avoided if the manager is aware of the types of rating errors and conscientiously focuses on performance and behaviors, not on the person. Watch out for these traps:

- **Halo Effect/Horns Effect.** The employee carries an aura of effectiveness that inflates or deflates rating; the manager believes the employee can do no wrong (Halo Effect). Or, the opposite applies and the manager believes the employee can do no right (Horns Effect).

- **Latest Behavior Effect.** The most recent behavior or accomplishment, positive or negative, is given more weighting than appropriate in the overall rating.

- **Guilt or Honor by Association Effect.** The employee is linked to another person, group, or project that influences how he or she is perceived, either negatively (Guilt by Association) or favorably (Honor by Association).

- **Rater Tendencies.** Ideally, all managers would rate the same performance in the same way just as, ideally, all baseball umpires would call the same pitch in the same way. We've all had teachers who were tough graders or easy graders. Managers, likewise, can be biased with a Strict Rating Tendency (a tough grader) or a Lenient Rating Tendency (an easy grader). Some display a Central Rating Tendency and avoid rating anyone high or low in an attempt to avoid controversy or confrontation. One of the best ways for rater tendencies to be addressed is by making each manager's rating distribution transparent to and reviewed by peers. When a peer group of managers share their rating distribution, managers who rate outside the norms will usually move closer to or within the norms over time.

- **Initial Impression Effect.** The employee made such a powerful first impression, positive or negative, that the effect lingers and carries over into ratings.

- **Spillover Effect.** Exceptionally strong or weak performance in one area unduly influences ratings in another area.

- **Status Effect.** A job title, educational pedigree, previous job experience, or some other factor inappropriately influences ratings.

- **Same As Me Effect/Different Than Me Effect.** The manager tends to rate employees with similar backgrounds or traits higher and those who are different lower.

Forced Distribution and Forced Ranking

Clear identification and differentiation of performance is critical to create a high-performance culture. But studies have repeatedly shown that managers generally fail in this regard and tend to significantly inflate ratings. To address this issue, many companies are adopting forced distribution or forced ranking systems. In a forced distribution system, a certain percentage of employees are rated in each category—for example, 20% identified as top performers, 70% as solid performers, and 10% as under-performers. In a forced ranking system, managers are required to rank order each employee in the workgroup.

Is a forced ranking system appropriate for your organization? To make that determination, start by reading Dick Grote's book, *Forced Ranking: Making Performance Management Work*. Some things to keep in mind:

- Pay attention to organizational culture. A forced ranking system won't work if the cultural norms are egalitarianism, lack of transparency, and defensiveness.

- Forced ranking systems will only work to the extent that peer discussions are deep, unbiased, and objective. In addition to a supportive culture, this requires integrity and trust, managerial courage, and skills in conflict management and sizing up people.

- Forced ranking systems are sabotaged by managers who tell their employees, "I rated you highly, but others moved you down." This can't be allowed. Again, managerial courage and conflict management skills are required.

Forced ranking systems are not for every organization. Research shows they are most effective in the first couple of years of implementation and then offer diminishing returns, so it's essential to modify the system to keep pace with organizational needs. Whether or not you adopt such a system, it's important to ensure the focal point of your performance management process is honest, meaningful conversations about performance that lead to differentiated ratings in the performance review.

Documenting the Review
Documentation of performance reviews has legal implications, and current laws and regulations, including state and local laws, should be consulted to ensure compliance. The high-level guidelines provided here are not intended to constitute legal advice.

- Ratings should be based on job content.

- Ratings should only address results and behaviors and never personality traits.

- Managers and supervisors should receive training and written instructions on delivering and documenting performance reviews.

- Employees should be given the right to review and comment in writing on the performance review documentation.

Linking to Consequences
Performance reviews should not be the only criteria used to determine pay raises, promotions, and terminations. In practice, they play a major role in these decisions in most organizations. For the link between performance reviews and consequences to work well, it should be well defined and made crystal clear for employees.

Most organizations have merit pay systems. Most don't work for two primary reasons: (1) Employees don't understand the system because it's mysterious at best or secretive at worst; and (2) Organizations don't do what they say they're going to do. If you're going to make 50% of merit bonuses dependent on organizational performance measured by a combination of factors that include return on assets, net new business growth, and customer loyalty, you'd better make sure employees understand how those things are measured and how they individually impact those measures. If you proclaim a desire to reward top performance by awarding 30% of the merit budget pool to the top 10% of performers and withhold all merit pay from the bottom 10% of performers, you better have managers with the courage to follow through and execute that plan. Tell employees how they will be rewarded, make sure they understand how to earn the bonus, and then pay it out like you said you would.

Reviewing Job Improvement

The guidelines provided in this book will lead to productive conversations about setting goals, providing feedback, and coaching. These are given in the context of performance management and improving job performance. While the guidelines are, for the most part, equally appropriate for discussions with employees about their personal and career development, we suggest you keep development discussions separate from the performance review.

It's hard enough for managers to be direct and focus on performance issues without having an escape hatch to easily divert the conversation to development and career path. Performance management discussions should focus on the job, on goal accomplishment, on work behaviors, and on ways to improve performance. Set aside other times that are dedicated for discussion of learning plans, development, and career advancement.

If you're separating job improvement discussions from development discussions, it follows then that 360° feedback should not be used in performance reviews. This is firmly supported by the research that overwhelmingly indicates 360° feedback is best limited to development and not tied to performance reviews, promotions, or compensation.

Mapping the 10 Universal Performance Dimensions to the 67 Leadership Competencies and Associated Remedies

81. Quantity of Output of Work

Quantity or amount of work produced personally or from a group or team on assignments/tasks/projects/products/or services without regard to any other factors like quality or timeliness of the work.

FOR INDIVIDUAL PERFORMANCE IMPROVEMENT IN THIS AREA, READ:

- **_FYI For Your Improvement™_ Chapters:**
  1. Action Oriented, 32. Learning on the Fly, 39. Organizing,
  51. Problem Solving, 53. Drive for Results, 81. Quantity of Output of Work

- **_FYI_ Specific Tip References: (Chapter Number - Tip Number)**
  Improvement: 52-3; 53-1, 2, 3, 4, 6, 7, 8, 9, 10
  Overuse: 17-3, 5; 33-3, 7; 41-7, 8, 9; 50-3; 51-1; 52-8

FOR MANAGER PERFORMANCE IMPROVEMENT IN THIS AREA, READ:

- **_FYI For Your Improvement™_ Chapters:**
  15. Customer Focus, 18. Delegation, 20. Directing Others, 27. Informing,
  35. Managing and Measuring Work, 36. Motivating Others, 39. Organizing,
  47. Planning, 50. Priority Setting, 53. Drive for Results, 65. Managing Vision and Purpose, 81. Quantity of Output of Work

- **_FYI_ Specific Tip References: (Chapter Number - Tip Number)**
  Improvement: 15-6, 8; 27-3; 35-1, 2; 36-1, 3; 39-2; 53-3; 65-1
  Overuse: 17-5; 41-5, 6, 7, 8; 50-3; 51-2; 53-5; 62-9; 118-1

FOR TEAM PERFORMANCE IMPROVEMENT IN THIS AREA, READ:

- **_FYI For Your Improvement™_ Chapters:**
  16. Timely Decision Making, 35. Managing and Measuring Work,
  39. Organizing, 47. Planning, 50. Priority Setting, 51. Problem Solving,
  53. Drive for Results, 81. Quantity of Output of Work

- **_FYI_ Specific Tip References: (Chapter Number - Tip Number)**
  Improvement: 52-3; 53-1, 2, 4, 5, 6, 7, 8, 9, 10
  Overuse: 17-3,5; 33-3, 7; 41-7, 8, 9; 50-3; 51-1; 52-8

Select one to three of the competencies listed below to use as a substitute for this Performance Management Dimension if you decide not to work on it directly.

SUBSTITUTES: 1,14,15,16,18,19,20,24,25,36,39,43,52,59,61,63

82. Timeliness of Delivery of Output

Timely delivery of goods and services in terms of schedules, deadlines, goals and targets without regard to other factors like quality and resourcefulness.

FOR INDIVIDUAL PERFORMANCE IMPROVEMENT IN THIS AREA, READ:

- **FYI For Your Improvement™ Chapters:**
  1. Action Oriented, 16. Timely Decision Making, 43. Perseverance,
  50. Priority Setting, 62. Time Management, 82. Timeliness of Delivery of Output

- **FYI Specific Tip References: (Chapter Number - Tip Number)**
  Improvement: 1-5, 7, 10; 16-1, 2, 3, 4, 8; 38-8; 52-3
  Overuse: 11-4; 17-3, 5; 33-3; 41-1, 7, 8, 9; 51-2, 3

FOR MANAGER PERFORMANCE IMPROVEMENT IN THIS AREA, READ:

- **FYI For Your Improvement™ Chapters:**
  1. Action Oriented, 16. Timely Decision Making, 20. Directing Others,
  35. Managing and Measuring Work, 36. Motivating Others, 39. Organizing,
  50. Priority Setting, 51. Problem Solving, 52. Process Management,
  53. Drive for Results, 82. Timeliness of Delivery of Output

- **FYI Specific Tip References: (Chapter Number - Tip Number)**
  Improvement: 1-5; 16-1, 3; 18-8; 20-3; 35-7; 36-1; 38-8; 43-1; 52-3
  Overuse: 17-5; 41-6, 7, 8; 50-3; 51-2, 3; 53-5; 62-9; 118-1

FOR TEAM PERFORMANCE IMPROVEMENT IN THIS AREA, READ:

- **FYI For Your Improvement™ Chapters:**
  1. Action Oriented, 16. Timely Decision Making, 35. Managing and Measuring Work, 50. Priority Setting, 62. Time Management, 82. Timeliness of Delivery of Output

- **FYI Specific Tip References: (Chapter Number - Tip Number)**
  Improvement: 1-5; 2-1,10; 16-1, 3; 35-1; 38-8; 43-1; 52-3; 53-6
  Overuse: 17-5; 33-3; 41-1, 7, 8, 9; 50-2; 51-2, 3; 62-9

Select one to three of the competencies listed below to use as a substitute for this Performance Management Dimension if you decide not to work on it directly.
SUBSTITUTES: 1,2,12,17,18,20,32,37,43,50,51,52,53,62

83. Quality of Work Output

The quality of goods and services produced in terms of errors, waste, and rework required to meet standards, not considering other things like timeliness or quantity.

FOR INDIVIDUAL PERFORMANCE IMPROVEMENT IN THIS AREA, READ:

- *FYI For Your Improvement*™ **Chapters:**
  15. Customer Focus, 17. Decision Quality, 24. Functional/Technical Skills, 51. Problem Solving, 63. Total Work Systems (TQM/ISO/Six Sigma), 83. Quality of Work Output

- *FYI* **Specific Tip References: (Chapter Number - Tip Number)**
  Improvement: 16-3; 51-1, 2, 3, 8; 52-3, 8; 63-1, 2, 7
  Overuse: 1-1, 3, 5; 2-1, 2, 7, 10; 16-8; 52-3, 8

FOR MANAGER PERFORMANCE IMPROVEMENT IN THIS AREA, READ:

- *FYI For Your Improvement*™ **Chapters:**
  17. Decision Quality, 18. Delegation, 20. Directing Others, 24. Functional/Technical Skills, 35. Managing and Measuring Work, 51. Problem Solving, 52. Process Management, 59. Managing Through Systems, 63. Total Work Systems (TQM/ISO/Six Sigma), 83. Quality of Work Output

- *FYI* **Specific Tip References: (Chapter Number - Tip Number)**
  Improvement: 17-3; 18-10; 35-2; 51-1, 2, 8; 52-3, 8; 63-1, 8
  Overuse: 1-1, 3, 5; 2-1, 2, 7, 10; 16-8; 52-3, 8

FOR TEAM PERFORMANCE IMPROVEMENT IN THIS AREA, READ:

- *FYI For Your Improvement*™ **Chapters:**
  15. Customer Focus, 17. Decision Quality, 35. Managing and Measuring Work, 51. Problem Solving, 63. Total Work Systems (TQM/ISO/Six Sigma), 83. Quality of Work Output

- *FYI* **Specific Tip References: (Chapter Number - Tip Number)**
  Improvement: 16-3; 35-2; 51-1, 2, 8; 52-3, 8; 63-1, 2, 8
  Overuse: 1-1, 3, 5; 2-1, 2, 7, 10; 16-8; 52-3, 8

Select one to three of the competencies listed below to use as a substitute for this Performance Management Dimension if you decide not to work on it directly.

SUBSTITUTES: 5,15,17,18,20,28,32,33,35,39,47,50,51,52,53,65

84. Use of Resources

The efficiency of use of time, money, materials and people to produce the required goods and services without considering other factors like timeliness or quality.

FOR INDIVIDUAL PERFORMANCE IMPROVEMENT IN THIS AREA, READ:

- *FYI For Your Improvement*™ **Chapters:**
  14. Creativity, 17. Decision Quality, 32. Learning on the Fly, 39. Organizing, 47. Planning, 50. Priority Setting, 63. Total Work Systems (TQM/ISO/Six Sigma), 84. Use of Resources

- *FYI* **Specific Tip References: (Chapter Number - Tip Number)**
  Improvement: 16-3; 39-1, 2, 3, 7; 47-7; 52-3; 62-3; 63-9, 10
  Overuse: 51-1, 2; 52-3, 8, 9; 53-1; 63-1, 2, 3, 8

FOR MANAGER PERFORMANCE IMPROVEMENT IN THIS AREA, READ:

- *FYI For Your Improvement*™ **Chapters:**
  32. Learning on the Fly, 36. Motivating Others, 37. Negotiating, 39. Organizing, 42. Peer Relationships, 50. Priority Setting, 51. Problem Solving, 52. Process Management, 84. Use of Resources

- *FYI* **Specific Tip References: (Chapter Number - Tip Number)**
  Improvement: 16-3; 35-2; 39-1, 2, 3; 47-7; 52-3, 7; 62-3; 63-10
  Overuse: 51-1, 2; 52-3, 8, 9; 53-1; 63-1, 2, 3, 8

FOR TEAM PERFORMANCE IMPROVEMENT IN THIS AREA, READ:

- *FYI For Your Improvement*™ **Chapters:**
  37. Negotiating, 39. Organizing, 47. Planning, 50. Priority Setting, 51. Problem Solving, 52. Process Management, 53. Drive for Results, 84. Use of Resources

- *FYI* **Specific Tip References: (Chapter Number - Tip Number)**
  Improvement: 16-3; 35-2; 39-1, 2, 3; 47-7; 52-3, 7; 62-3; 63-10
  Overuse: 51-1, 2; 52-3, 8, 9; 53-1; 63-1, 2, 3, 8

Select one to three of the competencies listed below to use as a substitute for this Performance Management Dimension if you decide not to work on it directly.
SUBSTITUTES: 5,15,17,18,20,24,32,33,35,39,47,50,51,58,59

85. Customer Impact/Value Added

The extent to which the goods and services produced meet the expectations of the internal and external customers.

FOR INDIVIDUAL PERFORMANCE IMPROVEMENT IN THIS AREA, READ:

- **FYI For Your Improvement™ Chapters:**
  1. Action Oriented, 15. Customer Focus, 17. Decision Quality, 24. Functional/Technical Skills, 53. Drive for Results, 63. Total Work Systems (TQM/ISO/Six Sigma), 85. Customer Impact/Value Added

- **FYI Specific Tip References: (Chapter Number - Tip Number)**
  Improvement: 15-1, 2, 3, 4, 8, 9; 33-7; 50-2, 3; 104-4
  Overuse: 12-7; 47-1, 7; 50-7; 53-1; 102-7; 105-2, 3, 4, 5

FOR MANAGER PERFORMANCE IMPROVEMENT IN THIS AREA, READ:

- **FYI For Your Improvement™ Chapters:**
  13. Confronting Direct Reports, 15. Customer Focus, 17. Decision Quality, 24. Functional/Technical Skills, 28. Innovation Management, 37. Negotiating, 50. Priority Setting, 58. Strategic Agility, 63. Total Work Systems (TQM/ISO/ Six Sigma), 85. Customer Impact/Value Added

- **FYI Specific Tip References: (Chapter Number - Tip Number)**
  Improvement: 13-2; 15-1, 2, 3, 4, 8, 9; 17-3; 28-1; 63-10
  Overuse: 12-7; 47-1; 50-2, 7; 53-1; 102-7; 105-2, 3, 4, 5

FOR TEAM PERFORMANCE IMPROVEMENT IN THIS AREA, READ:

- **FYI For Your Improvement™ Chapters:**
  14. Creativity, 15. Customer Focus, 28. Innovation Management, 50. Priority Setting, 51. Problem Solving, 53. Drive for Results, 63. Total Work Systems (TQM/ISO/Six Sigma), 85. Customer Impact/Value Added

- **FYI Specific Tip References: (Chapter Number - Tip Number)**
  Improvement: 14-1; 15-1, 2, 3, 4, 8, 9; 28-1; 50-2, 3
  Overuse: 12-7; 47-1; 50-2, 7; 53-1; 102-7; 105-2, 3, 4, 5

Select one to three of the competencies listed below to use as a substitute for this Performance Management Dimension if you decide not to work on it directly.

SUBSTITUTES: 1,3,9,16,24,27,31,32,33,38,39,43,47,48,50,51,52,53,61,63

86. Freedom From Unplanned Support
The amount and intensity of supervision and support necessary to perform up to standard.

FOR INDIVIDUAL PERFORMANCE IMPROVEMENT IN THIS AREA, READ:

- *FYI For Your Improvement*™ **Chapters:**
  1. Action Oriented, 17. Decision Quality, 24. Functional/Technical Skills,
  47. Planning, 50. Priority Setting, 53. Drive for Results, 57. Standing Alone,
  62. Time Management, 86. Freedom from Unplanned Support

- *FYI* **Specific Tip References: (Chapter Number - Tip Number)**
  Improvement: 1-4; 12-5; 16-3, 4, 10; 57-3, 5, 8, 10; 62-9
  Overuse: 3-3, 6, 9; 27-3; 31-1; 33-6, 9; 38-4; 42-6; 53-6

FOR MANAGER PERFORMANCE IMPROVEMENT IN THIS AREA, READ:

- *FYI For Your Improvement*™ **Chapters:**
  2. Dealing with Ambiguity, 9. Command Skills, 18. Delegation, 27. Informing,
  35. Managing and Measuring Work, 47. Planning, 56. Sizing Up People,
  57. Standing Alone, 59. Managing Through Systems, 86. Freedom from
  Unplanned Support

- *FYI* **Specific Tip References: (Chapter Number - Tip Number)**
  Improvement: 2-1; 9-1; 12-7; 18-2, 3; 35-1, 7; 47-1; 56-5; 59-6
  Overuse: 3-9; 27-3; 31-1; 33-6, 9; 38-4; 42-5, 6; 53-6; 101-4

FOR TEAM PERFORMANCE IMPROVEMENT IN THIS AREA, READ:

- *FYI For Your Improvement*™ **Chapters:**
  2. Dealing with Ambiguity, 9. Command Skills, 16. Timely Decision Making,
  35. Managing and Measuring Work, 50. Priority Setting,
  52. Process Management, 54. Self-Development, 57. Standing Alone,
  86. Freedom from Unplanned Support

- *FYI* **Specific Tip References: (Chapter Number - Tip Number)**
  Improvement: 1-4; 2-1; 12-5; 16-3, 4, 10; 57-5, 8, 10; 62-9
  Overuse: 3-9; 17-8; 27-3; 31-1; 33-6, 9; 38-4; 42-6; 51-5; 53-6

Select one to three of the competencies listed below to use as a substitute for this Performance Management Dimension if you decide not to work on it directly.
SUBSTITUTES: 1,9,12,16,27,34,37,38,39,43,47,48,50,53,57

87. Team/Unit Contribution

Unrelated to personal or group performance, is helpful to others in the unit or organization in getting work done or setting a tone of cooperation.

FOR INDIVIDUAL PERFORMANCE IMPROVEMENT IN THIS AREA, READ:

- **_FYI For Your Improvement_™ Chapters:**
  3. Approachability, 27. Informing, 33. Listening, 42. Peer Relationships,
  60. Building Effective Teams, 87. Team/Unit Contribution

- **_FYI_ Specific Tip References: (Chapter Number - Tip Number)**
  Improvement: 27-3; 31-2, 5; 33-7; 38-4; 42-1, 2, 4, 5, 6
  Overuse: 12-7; 37-10; 50-1, 2; 53-1; 62-3, 9; 105-2, 4, 5

FOR MANAGER PERFORMANCE IMPROVEMENT IN THIS AREA, READ:

- **_FYI For Your Improvement_™ Chapters:**
  3. Approachability, 31. Interpersonal Savvy, 33. Listening, 36. Motivating Others,
  38. Organizational Agility, 42. Peer Relationships, 60. Building Effective Teams,
  65. Managing Vision and Purpose, 87. Team/Unit Contribution

- **_FYI_ Specific Tip References: (Chapter Number - Tip Number)**
  Improvement: 27-3; 31-2, 5; 33-7; 38-4; 42-1, 5, 6; 53-6; 65-2
  Overuse: 12-7; 37-10; 50-1, 2; 53-1; 62-3, 9; 105-2, 4, 5

FOR TEAM PERFORMANCE IMPROVEMENT IN THIS AREA, READ:

- **_FYI For Your Improvement_™ Chapters:**
  31. Interpersonal Savvy, 33. Listening, 37. Negotiating,
  38. Organizational Agility, 42. Peer Relationships, 87. Team/Unit Contribution

- **_FYI_ Specific Tip References: (Chapter Number - Tip Number)**
  Improvement: 27-3; 31-2, 5; 33-7; 38-4; 42-1, 4, 5, 6; 53-6
  Overuse: 12-7; 37-10; 50-1, 2; 53-1; 62-3, 9; 105-2, 4, 5

Select one to three of the competencies listed below to use as a substitute for this Performance Management Dimension if you decide not to work on it directly.

SUBSTITUTES: 3,12,21,27,31,33,36,38,41,42,48,60,64

88. Productive Work Habits

The extent to which overall work style is effective and productive in terms of time management, setting objectives and priorities, and following up on commitments across a variety of work challenges.

FOR INDIVIDUAL PERFORMANCE IMPROVEMENT IN THIS AREA, READ:

- **_FYI For Your Improvement_™ Chapters:**
  1. Action Oriented, 39. Organizing, 47. Planning, 50. Priority Setting, 62. Time Management, 63. Total Work Systems (TQM/ISO/Six Sigma), 88. Productive Work Habits

- **_FYI_ Specific Tip References: (Chapter Number - Tip Number)**
  Improvement: 16-3; 47-1, 3, 5, 8; 50-3, 7; 52-3, 8; 62-3
  Overuse: 1-5; 2-1, 2, 7, 10; 16-8; 51-3, 8; 101-2; 118-8

FOR MANAGER PERFORMANCE IMPROVEMENT IN THIS AREA, READ:

- **_FYI For Your Improvement_™ Chapters:**
  13. Confronting Direct Reports, 27. Informing, 35. Managing and Measuring Work, 47. Planning, 50. Priority Setting, 62. Time Management, 88. Productive Work Habits

- **_FYI_ Specific Tip References: (Chapter Number - Tip Number)**
  Improvement: 13-2; 16-3; 35-1, 7; 47-1; 50-3, 7; 52-8; 62-3; 105-2
  Overuse: 1-5; 2-1, 2, 7, 10; 16-8; 51-3, 8; 101-2; 118-8

FOR TEAM PERFORMANCE IMPROVEMENT IN THIS AREA, READ:

- **_FYI For Your Improvement_™ Chapters:**
  39. Organizing, 47. Planning, 50. Priority Setting, 52. Process Management, 53. Drive for Results, 88. Productive Work Habits

- **_FYI_ Specific Tip References: (Chapter Number - Tip Number)**
  Improvement: 16-3; 47-1, 3, 5, 8; 50-3, 7; 52-3, 8; 62-3
  Overuse: 1-5; 2-1, 2, 7, 10; 16-8; 51-3, 8; 101-2; 118-8

Select one to three of the competencies listed below to use as a substitute for this Performance Management Dimension if you decide not to work on it directly.

SUBSTITUTES: 1,18,20,35,36,39,47,50,52,53,60,62

89. Adding Skills and Capabilities

The extent to which any capabilities were added to the current portfolio of skills, attitudes, and knowledge in order to get work done and build for the future.

FOR INDIVIDUAL PERFORMANCE IMPROVEMENT IN THIS AREA, READ:

- **FYI For Your Improvement™ Chapters:**
  6. Career Ambition, 32. Learning on the Fly, 54. Self-Development,
  61. Technical Learning, 89. Adding Skills and Capabilities

- **FYI Specific Tip References: (Chapter Number - Tip Number)**
  Improvement: 1-6; 6-3, 8; 54-1, 2, 3, 10; 55-9, 10; 101-6
  Overuse: 6-3, 5; 50-2, 6; 53-1; 54-7; 55-1, 3; 62-3; 118-1

FOR MANAGER PERFORMANCE IMPROVEMENT IN THIS AREA, READ:

- **FYI For Your Improvement™ Chapters:**
  5. Business Acumen, 6. Career Ambition, 13. Confronting Direct Reports,
  19. Developing Direct Reports and Others, 36. Motivating Others,
  54. Self-Development, 55. Self-Knowledge, 65. Managing Vision and Purpose,
  89. Adding Skills and Capabilities

- **FYI Specific Tip References: (Chapter Number - Tip Number)**
  Improvement: 1-6; 5-6; 6-3; 13-2; 19-7; 36-2; 51-8; 54-10; 58-4; 118-8
  Overuse: 6-3; 50-1, 2, 6, 7; 53-1; 54-7; 62-1, 3; 118-1

FOR TEAM PERFORMANCE IMPROVEMENT IN THIS AREA, READ:

- **FYI For Your Improvement™ Chapters:**
  5. Business Acumen, 13. Confronting Direct Reports, 15. Customer Focus,
  19. Developing Direct Reports and Others, 28. Innovation Management,
  55. Self-Knowledge, 58. Strategic Agility, 89. Adding Skills and Capabilities

- **FYI Specific Tip References: (Chapter Number - Tip Number)**
  Improvement: 1-6; 5-6; 15-3; 19-4; 28-1, 10; 51-8; 55-3; 58-4; 101-2
  Overuse: 6-3; 50-1, 2, 6, 7; 53-1; 54-7; 62-1, 3; 118-1

Select one to three of the competencies listed below to use as a substitute for this Performance Management Dimension if you decide not to work on it directly.
SUBSTITUTES: 1,6,18,19,32,33,44,45,54,55,61

90. Alignment and Compliance: Walking the Talk

The extent to which this person behaves in a way that is aligned with the values, culture and mission of the organization without regard to how well they do their work.

FOR INDIVIDUAL PERFORMANCE IMPROVEMENT IN THIS AREA, READ:

- **FYI For Your Improvement™ Chapters:**
  12. Conflict Management, 22. Ethics and Values, 33. Listening, 38. Organizational Agility, 40. Dealing with Paradox, 41. Patience, 45. Personal Learning, 48. Political Savvy, 90. Alignment and Compliance: Walking the Talk

- **FYI Specific Tip References: (Chapter Number - Tip Number)**
  Improvement: 12-1,5; 22-2, 4, 5, 9; 41-4; 45-2,10; 65-10
  Overuse: 1-5; 14-1; 51-1, 8; 55-3; 57-1, 2, 8; 101-4, 6

FOR MANAGER PERFORMANCE IMPROVEMENT IN THIS AREA, READ:

- **FYI For Your Improvement™ Chapters:**
  12. Conflict Management, 20. Directing Others, 22. Ethics and Values, 25. Hiring and Staffing, 27. Informing, 33. Listening, 36. Motivating Others, 38. Organizational Agility, 39. Organizing, 40. Dealing with Paradox, 49. Presentation Skills, 65. Managing Vision and Purpose, 90. Alignment and Compliance: Walking the Talk

- **FYI Specific Tip References: (Chapter Number - Tip Number)**
  Improvement: 12-1, 5; 22-2, 4, 5; 38-4; 42-5; 45-2; 65-7, 10
  Overuse: 1-5; 14-1; 51-1, 8; 55-3; 57-1, 2, 8; 101-4, 6

FOR TEAM PERFORMANCE IMPROVEMENT IN THIS AREA, READ:

- **FYI For Your Improvement™ Chapters:**
  12. Conflict Management, 22. Ethics and Values, 33. Listening, 38. Organizational Agility, 40. Dealing with Paradox, 41. Patience, 42. Peer Relationships, 45. Personal Learning, 90. Alignment and Compliance: Walking the Talk

- **FYI Specific Tip References: (Chapter Number - Tip Number)**
  Improvement: 12-1; 22-2, 4, 5; 38-4; 42-5, 6; 45-2, 9; 65-10
  Overuse: 1-5; 14-1; 51-1, 8; 55-3; 57-1, 2, 8; 101-4, 6

Select one to three of the competencies listed below to use as a substitute for this Performance Management Dimension if you decide not to work on it directly.
SUBSTITUTES: 2,3,4,11,17,22,26,29,31,40,41,48,53

APPENDIX G: BEHAVIORALLY ANCHORED RATING SCALES (BARS) FOR PERFORMANCE MANAGEMENT

The 10 Performance Dimensions are part of the Lominger LEADERSHIP ARCHITECT® Competency Library. Each Dimension represents a key aspect of how performance is achieved and has a corresponding ten-point behaviorally anchored rating scale (BARS). The Dimensions and BARS, in addition to being listed here, are available in a card deck format, the Performance Management Architect® Sort Cards, to facilitate training or group processes. The *PMA Quick Reference Guide* provides guidelines for using the PMA Sort Cards.

81. Quantity of Output of Work

Quantity or amount of work produced personally or from a group or team on assignments/tasks/projects/products/or services without regard to any other factors like quality or timeliness of the work.

10. Overused: Rating 7 (still considered a strength at a low level): Is so high that sometimes quality suffers because work is so intense and the pace is so fast. Can be so single-mindedly focused on getting the most work out possible, that all other matters including concern for self and others suffer. Even though the work gets done, at what price? May be a workaholic.

9. Exceeds(+): Is simply amazing. Time after time, no matter how high the production or output goals are set, more is produced than is expected in all areas. Almost always number one in productivity; defines hard work for the rest.

8. Exceeds: Is significant. Keeps meeting all production or output goals and exceeds a few, no matter how high the standard. Beats most other comparable people or groups in productivity.

7. Exceeds(–): Is notable. Almost all production or output goals are met. Usually outproduces most other similar people or groups. Important goals are always met. If a goal is missed, the miss is on the less important and then not by much.

6. Meets(+): Is slightly more productive than most others. Most production or output goals are met; a few are missed, but not by much.

5. Meets: Is acceptable and about like most other people or similar groups. Most production goals are met; a few may be missed. Work output is at standard.

4. Meets(–): Is slightly behind others on what's acceptable or expected. Some significant goals or targets are missed, or the goals/targets are not quite up to par; they miss, but not by much.

3. Misses(+): Lags behind other equivalent people or groups and does not fully meet expectations. Significant goals are missed and productivity in general is always slightly lower than most others. A few goals are met, but some are missed.

2. Misses: Is well below expectations. Although a few production goals and targets are met, most others are not. The level of productivity is inconsistent, sporadic, or just low.

1. Misses(–): Is unacceptable. All production goals and targets are missed by a significant amount. Just not able to get the work out.

82. Timeliness of Delivery of Output

Timely delivery of goods and services in terms of schedules, deadlines, goals and targets without regard to other factors like quality and resourcefulness.

10. Overused: Rating 7 (still considered a strength at a low level): Is so committed to meeting deadlines and getting things done on time that things get too intense. As the delivery target comes closer, things like morale or quality or costs suffer at the last minute. Getting it done on time becomes too important.

9. Exceeds(+): Is always the first or among the first to finish. Even unreasonable or difficult time targets and goals are met and some are actually exceeded. Delivers the goods well before they are due. The fastest around. Sets the speed and pace standard for the rest.

8. Exceeds: Always finishes everything on time. Even difficult time targets and goals are met. Among the fastest and most timely performers around.

7. Exceeds(–): Usually finishes the most important things on time. The most important time targets are always met. May be a bit late on some time targets, but not by much. Faster than the majority of comparable people or groups around.

6. Meets(+): Produces most work on time and timeliness is slightly above standard. Misses a few time deadlines. A bit more timely than most other comparable people or groups.

5. Meets: Produces most work on time and timeliness is acceptable and at standard. Meets deadlines on most work; may miss on a few. About as timely as most other comparable people or groups.

4. Meets(–): Produces most work on time and timeliness is acceptable but a bit lower than standard. Meets some deadlines and misses on some. A little less timely than most other people or groups.

3. Misses(+): Has trouble finishing things on time. Misses some deadlines by a notable amount and just meets standard for others. Slower than a lot of other comparable people or groups.

2. Misses: Is always among the last to finish. Delivery is inconsistent, sporadic, or just late. Misses important deadlines by a significant amount and barely meets standard for others. Among the slowest people or groups around.

1. Misses(–): Is always the last to finish and always late with work. Misses most if not all deadlines by a significant amount and even with additional time, only meets minimal standards.

83. Quality of Work Output

The quality of goods and services produced in terms of errors, waste, and rework required to meet standards, not considering other things like timeliness or quantity.

10. Overused: Rating 7 (still considered a strength at a low level): Produces very high-quality work, but perfectionism leads to things like lower productivity, some missed deadlines, using too many resources to finish or taking too long to get there. Quality standards exceed what's reasonable.

9. Exceeds(+): Always produces work that is totally error free the first time with no waste or rework. The work is used as the quality standard for everyone else to shoot for.

8. Exceeds: Produces work that is mostly error free with little waste or rework. The quality of the work is always among the best.

7. Exceeds(–): Produces work that is usually error free with some waste or rework. The quality of the work is better than that of most others.

6. Meets(+): Produces work that is of better-than-average quality—most is error free, some with a few errors and rework, and some occasionally not quite up to standard with some waste on the way to getting things done.

5. Meets: Produces work that is of reasonable quality—most is acceptable, with a few errors and rework. Occasionally not quite up to standard with some waste of time or resources on the way to getting things done. Performs at the quality standard.

4. Meets(–): Produces work that is slightly off the quality standard—some is fine, but some has a few errors and rework, and some is not up to standard with noticeable waste on the way to getting things done.

3. Misses(+): Produces work that is below the quality standard, contains notable and careless errors. Usually requires rework before it can be used and then barely meets average minimum quality standards or specifications.

2. Misses: Produces work that is well below the quality standard, contains frequent and careless errors. Usually requires rework before it can be used and then sometimes doesn't meet minimum quality standards or specifications. The quality of work is inconsistent, sporadic, or just plain poor.

1. Misses(–): Produces work that is far from the quality standard, contains unacceptable and sloppy errors. Always requires rework before it can be used and then doesn't meet minimum quality standards or specifications.

84. Use of Resources

The efficiency of use of time, money, materials and people to produce the required goods and services without considering other factors like timeliness or quality.

10. Overused: Rating 7 (still considered a strength at a low level): Always comes in on or even below budget, sometimes at the price of lower quantity or quality. So concerned with making or beating the budget plan that other things suffer. May cut corners on costs so tight that there are problems later in the work flow. Even though everything is on or under budget, at what price?

9. Exceeds(+): Always comes in significantly under budget in all areas. Always uses fewer resources in terms of time, material, money and people than any other comparable people or groups. Gets more things done with less. A model of resourcefulness.

8. Exceeds: Always comes in under budget in all areas. Always uses fewer resources in terms of time, material, money and people than most other comparable people or groups. Always finds ways to get more done with less.

7. Exceeds(–): Always comes in under budget in some areas and is right on target for the rest. Uses fewer resources in terms of time, material, money and people than most other comparable people or groups.

6. Meets(+): Always comes in right on budget, with efficient and as-planned use of materials and people. A bit more resourceful than most comparable people or groups.

5. Meets: Comes in on budget, with efficient and as-planned use of materials and people. Some work may come in over budget. About as resourceful as most comparable people or groups.

4. Meets(–): Produces some work that comes in on budget, with efficient and as-planned use of materials and people, but some work doesn't come in on budget. A little bit less resourceful than other comparable people or groups.

3. Misses(+): Is usually over budget on everything or significantly over budget on some and on budget on others. Uses resources inefficiently and even with additional resources, just meets minimum standards. Wastes time, money, material and people's productivity.

2. Misses: Is always over budget in most areas. Uses resources inefficiently and even with additional resources, barely meets minimum standards. Efficiency with resources is inconsistent, sporadic, or just plain excessive. Wastes time, money, material and people's productivity.

84. Use of Resources (continued)

1. Misses(–): Is always considerably over budget across-the-board. Uses resources inefficiently and even with additional resources, doesn't meet minimum standards. Has trouble projecting what things are going to cost. Whatever the projection, wastes time, money, material and people's productivity getting there.

85. Customer Impact/Value Added

The extent to which the goods and services produced meet the expectations of the internal and external customers.

10. Overused: Rating 7 (still considered a strength at a low level): Is overly committed to produce goods and services that consistently meet and exceed the standards and expectations of internal and external customers. Uses too many resources to deliver, loses sight of other important goals and objectives, and becomes an unreasonable advocate for customers at the expense of other organizational values and policies. Gives the customer too much for what the organization receives in return. The customer is always happy, but at what price?

9. Exceeds(+): Always exceeds the expectations and standards for internal and external customers. Always finds ways to delight and surprise customers with goods and services that are better than what they asked for or expected. Always out ahead of customers, anticipating needs even the customers don't yet realize. The model for pleasing customers.

8. Exceeds: Produces goods and services that consistently meet and sometimes exceed the standards and expectations of internal and external customers. Always up-to-date about customer needs and expectations. The feedback from customers is almost always positive.

7. Exceeds(–): Produces goods and services that consistently meet and once in a while exceed the standards and expectations of internal and external customers. Usually up-to-date about customer needs and expectations, and customer feedback is mostly positive.

6. Meets(+): Produces goods and services that consistently meet the standards and expectations of internal and external customers. Usually up-to-date about customer needs and expectations. Customers have no complaints.

5. Meets: Produces goods and services that usually meet the normal standards of internal and external customers. Most customers are happy, with a few customer complaints and some rework is necessary to make all customers happy.

4. Meets(–): Produces goods and services that mostly meet the normal standards of internal and external customers, but some efforts miss the mark by a little. There are some complaints and some rework is necessary to make the customers happy.

3. Misses(+): Produces goods and services that sometimes meet but sometimes miss the minimum standards and expectations of internal and external customers by a notable amount. There are complaints and rework is necessary to keep the customers happy.

85. Customer Impact/Value Added (continued)

2. Misses: Produces goods and services that don't meet the minimum standards and expectations of internal and external customers. Inconsistent, sporadic, or just lacking in meeting customer standards. There are steady complaints and extensive rework is necessary to keep customers minimally happy.

1. Misses(–): Produces goods and services that don't meet the minimum standards and expectations of internal and external customers. There are frequent complaints and extensive rework is necessary just to keep the customers, much less keep them happy.

86. Freedom From Unplanned Support

The amount and intensity of supervision and support necessary to perform up to standard.

10. Overused: Rating 7 (still considered a strength at a low level): Is so driven to work independently that they are unreasonable loners. Doesn't want any help, goes own way and works on own objectives. May waste time and resources working on the wrong things or in the wrong way.

9. Exceeds(+): Always performs up to standard or beyond on their own. Needs no support from bosses and other sources and needs no unplanned guidance or help. As a proportion of help or support available, takes up the least amount compared to comparable people or groups. Independent, self-starting, totally self-sufficient.

8. Exceeds: Usually performs up to standard or a bit beyond on their own. Takes up minimal support from bosses and other sources and needs little unplanned guidance or help. As a proportion of help available, takes up much less support than most other comparable people or groups.

7. Exceeds(–): Performs up to standard on their own. Takes up some support time from bosses and other sources, but as a proportion of help available, takes up less support than most other comparable people or groups.

6. Meets(+): Needs a little less than the usual amount of help and guidance from bosses and others to be able to consistently perform up to standard. As a proportion of help available, takes up a little less support than average.

5. Meets: Performs up to standard with the usual or reasonable amount of support, help, and guidance from bosses and others. As a proportion of help available, takes up just their fair share.

4. Meets(–): Needs a little more than the usual amount of help and guidance from bosses and others to be able to perform up to standard. As a proportion of help available, takes up a little more support than average.

3. Misses(+): Needs significantly more than average support and resources from bosses and others to meet minimum standards. Takes more maintenance and support than most comparable people or groups to be able to contribute up to standard.

2. Misses: Needs a significant amount of unplanned support and resources, and a disproportionate amount of guidance from bosses and others. Can only perform up to minimum standards with significant assistance. Takes a lot of maintenance and support just to be minimally contributing. Because so much attention is required, other people or groups suffer by getting less than they need.

86. Freedom From Unplanned Support (continued)

1. Misses(–): Needs an extensive amount of unplanned support and a disproportionate amount of guidance from bosses and others. Doesn't perform up to minimum standards. Takes a lot of maintenance and support just to be minimally contributing. Needs a tremendous percentage of the available resources, leaving other people or groups with less-than-adequate support.

87. Team/Unit Contribution

Unrelated to personal or group performance, is helpful to others in the unit or organization in getting work done or setting a tone of cooperation.

10. Overused: Rating 7 (still considered a strength at a low level): Is such a team player that own performance sometimes suffers. Takes too much time and energy helping others succeed. Sometimes runs out of time and resources for own work. While they certainly help others do their work, at what price?

9. Exceeds(+): Is always helpful to the rest of the team or to other units in addition to getting their own work done. Always the first to volunteer to put their priorities aside and help others succeed. What's theirs is yours if you need it. Will share resources and spend whatever time is necessary if it's for the good of the team or organization. The model of sharing, caring, and cooperation.

8. Exceeds: Is almost always helpful to the rest of the team or to other units in addition to getting their own work done. Among the first to volunteer to put their priorities aside and help others succeed. What's theirs is yours if they don't need it. Shares most anything they have if it's for the good of the team or organization.

7. Exceeds(–): Is more helpful than most others in assisting the rest of the team or other units to succeed. Freely shares resources and information when there is time.

6. Meets(+): Is a little more helpful to the rest of the team or other units than most comparable people or groups in getting their work done or in cooperating with them. Willing to share resources and information when asked.

5. Meets: Is usually helpful to the rest of the team or other units in getting their work done or in cooperating with them. About as helpful as most comparable people or groups.

4. Meets(–): Is a little less helpful than average to the rest of the team or other units in getting their work done or in cooperating with them. Sometimes resists sharing resources and information or taking time when they're busy.

3. Misses(+): Is seldom helpful to the rest of the team or other units in getting their work done or in cooperating with anyone. Can chill the efforts of others by only reluctantly getting involved or helping others.

2. Misses: Is rarely helpful to the rest of the team or other units in getting their work done or in cooperating with anyone. May chill the efforts of others by hesitating to get involved or even refusing to help. Withholds resources and information from others. Others complain from time to time about the lack of cooperation from this individual/ manager/team.

87. Team/Unit Contribution (continued)

1. Misses(–): Is not at all helpful to the rest of the team or other units in getting their work done or in cooperating with anyone. Mostly chills the efforts of others by resisting getting involved or helping others. Purposefully withholds important resources and information. Has no interest in helping others perform. The target of complaints from others.

88. Productive Work Habits

The extent to which overall work style is effective and productive in terms of time management, setting objectives and priorities, and following up on commitments across a variety of work challenges.

10. Overused: Rating 7 (still considered a strength at a low level): Is so obsessed with doing things in a planned and orderly manner, that the work is sometimes late or exceeds even reasonable quality standards. Easily thrown off balance by the unexpected and doesn't adjust well to change. Excessively compulsive about doing everything in an organized way. Although everything does get done right, at what price?

9. Exceeds(+): Is extremely efficient in planning and executing work. Expertly scopes out the work, creates the single most efficient workflow and processes, and obtains and assigns exactly the right resources that fit each step. Because of this, there is no challenge that comes their way that they can't plan for and handle. Always does things right the first time. A model of effective and efficient work habits.

8. Exceeds: Is very efficient in planning and executing work. Accurately scopes out the work, creates efficient workflow and processes, and assigns resources that fit each step. Because of this, there are few challenges that come their way that they can't handle. Consistently outperforms most other comparable people or groups because of excellence at planning, priority setting, time management, and execution.

7. Exceeds(–): Is efficient in planning and executing work. Scopes out the work, creates efficient workflow and processes, and assigns resources that fit each step. Usually outperforms other comparable people or groups because of resourceful planning, priority setting, and execution.

6. Meets(+): Is consistently productive and organized at setting appropriate objectives, setting priorities, managing time, and getting the work out. Follows through almost all of the time. A bit better than many other comparable people or groups.

5. Meets: Is reasonably productive and organized at getting the work out, setting appropriate objectives, managing time, and setting priorities. Follows through most of the time. Like most other comparable people or groups.

4. Meets(–): Is usually productive and organized at work, setting objectives, managing time, and setting priorities. Follows through some of the time. Slightly below the standard set by comparable people or groups.

3. Misses(+): Is not very orderly in approach to work. Works on whatever comes up, gets easily diverted into less productive tasks. Follow-through is spotty. Wastes a lot of energy and time due to being disorganized.

88. Productive Work Habits (continued)

2. Misses: Is disorganized and unproductive in approach to work. Works on whatever comes up first, doesn't set objectives. Follow-through is spotty. Does not follow orderly processes in most things. Approach to being effective and efficient is inconsistent, sporadic, or just below standard.

1. Misses(–): Is very disorganized and unproductive in approach to work. Works on whatever emergency comes up. Either doesn't set objectives or changes them too often. Follow-through is inconsistent and unacceptable. Does not follow orderly processes in anything and has unacceptable work habits.

89. Adding Skills and Capabilities

The extent to which any capabilities were added to the current portfolio of skills, attitudes, and knowledge in order to get work done and build for the future.

10. Overused: Rating 7 (still considered a strength at a low level): Spends so much time building skills and capabilities for tomorrow that they don't focus enough on the day-to-day work. Sometimes works on new skills that turn out to be only marginally helpful later.

9. Exceeds(+): Eagerly learns new skills and capabilities to improve themselves for the present and the future. Makes learning new skills and capabilities an equal priority to getting today's work done. Always much more and better skilled at the end of the year than at the beginning. Constantly building personal/team value. The model of a commitment to continuous improvement.

8. Exceeds: Readily learns new skills and capabilities to improve themselves for the present and the future. Seeks out new skills and knowledge, and builds the opportunity to learn into the daily routine. Always better skilled at the end of the year than at the beginning. Strives to build added value.

7. Exceeds(–): Comfortably learns new skills and capabilities to improve for the future. Seeks out opportunities to learn new skills and knowledge. Usually more skilled at the end of the year than at the beginning.

6. Meets(+): Shows a little more interest in learning new skills and knowledge than comparable others do. If it fits within the scope of the work, they will pursue. Has some interest in building future skills. Has a few more skills at the end of the year than at the beginning.

5. Meets: Has about as much interest in learning new skills and knowledge as comparable others do. If it fits in with the work, will learn when the opportunity is there. Generally keeps up with near-term new skill requirements. Shows mild interest in building future skills.

4. Meets(–): Is a little less interested in learning new skills and knowledge than comparable others. If it fits in with current work, learns when challenged to learn. Does not often seek new learning.

3. Misses(+): Has less interest than comparable others in learning and building new skills and knowledge. Concentrates on day-to-day work and doesn't expend much effort building skills for the future. Has about the same skills at the end of the year as at the beginning.

89. Adding Skills and Capabilities (continued)

2. Misses: Has little interest in learning and building new skills and knowledge. Content with current skill level. Slowly getting out-of-date and performance is beginning to suffer.

1. Misses(–): Has no interest in learning and building new skills and knowledge for today's job, much less future jobs. Stuck in a comfort zone. Getting out-of-date and performance is suffering.

90. Alignment and Compliance: Walking the Talk

The extent to which this person behaves in a way that is aligned with the values, culture and mission of the organization without regard to how well they do their work.

10. Overused: Rating 7 (still considered a strength at a low level): Is so dedicated to doing it the organization's way that judgment sometimes gets clouded. Only sees things one way and sometimes misses important exceptions that should be made. May be so compliant with organizational values and culture that decision making, innovation, and risk taking are stalled.

9. Exceeds(+): Is the gold standard for walking the organization talk. Truly believes in doing things the organization's way aligned with the values, culture and mission, and is looked upon by others as the model of success the right way. Always operates with mission and values in mind and encourages others to do the same.

8. Exceeds: Is on the values mark. Believes in and follows the organization way. Goes beyond other people or groups to align behavior with the values and mission of the organization.

7. Exceeds(–): Is aligned with the vast majority of the key tenets of the values and mission of the organization. Does things the organization's way and in line with the culture most of the time.

6. Meets(+): Is slightly more in alignment with doing things the organization's way than others. Behavior is generally aligned with the values, culture and mission of the organization.

5. Meets: Is in reasonable alignment with the organization's values and mission (like most other people or groups). Much of the time, with a few exceptions, does things in line with the culture and organizational preferences.

4. Meets(–): Is slightly less likely to behave in alignment with the organization's values and mission than others. Sometimes tests the borders of the right way to do things.

3. Misses(+): Is sometimes in alignment with what others expect, but deviates from time to time, insisting that they have a better way. Clashes with the organizational culture more than others.

2. Misses: Is mostly out of line with the values, culture and mission of the organization. Insists on doing things differently from others. Although they might get the work out, they rock the values boat.

1. Misses(–): Is always out of line with the organization's values, culture and mission. A real maverick. They always do things their own way regardless of the norms and preferences of the organization.

SUGGESTED READINGS FOR PERFORMANCE MANAGEMENT

Chingos, P. T. (2002). *Paying for performance: A guide to compensation management* (2nd ed.). New York, NY: John Wiley & Sons, Inc.

Daniels, A. C. (2000). *Bringing out the best in people: How to apply the astonishing power of positive reinforcement.* New York, NY: McGraw-Hill.

Eichinger, R. W., Lombardo, M. M., & Stiber, A. (2006). *Broadband talent management: Paths to improvement.* Minneapolis, MN: Lominger International: A Korn/Ferry Company.

Grote, D. (1996). *The complete guide to performance appraisal.* New York, NY: AMACOM/American Management Association.

Grote, D. (2002). *The performance appraisal question and answer book: A survival guide for managers.* New York, NY: AMACOM/American Management Association.

Grote, D. (2005). *Forced ranking: Making performance management work.* Boston, MA: Harvard Business School Press.

Huselid, M. A., & Becker, B. E. (2005). *The workforce scorecard: Managing human capital to execute strategy.* Boston, MA: Harvard Business School Press.

Kaplan, R. S., & Norton, D. P. (1996). T*he balanced scorecard: Translating strategy into action.* Boston, MA: Harvard Business School Press.

Kaplan, R. S., & Norton, D. P. (2001). Building a strategy-focused organization. *Ivey Business Journal, 65*(5), 12-19.

Lombardo, M. M., & Eichinger, R. W. (2005). *The leadership machine* (3rd ed.). Minneapolis, MN: Lominger International: A Korn/Ferry Company.

Lawler, E. (1996). *From the ground up: Six principles for building the new logic corporation.* San Francisco, CA: Jossey-Bass.

Lawler, E. E., III., & Lawler, E. E. (2003). *Treat people right: How organizations and employees can create a win/win relationship to achieve high performance at all levels.* San Francisco, CA: Jossey-Bass.

Max, D., & Bacal, R. (2002). *Perfect phrases for performance reviews: Hundreds of ready-to-use phrases that describe your employees' performance.* New York, NY: McGraw-Hill.

Ulrich, D., & Brockbank, W. (2005). *The HR value proposition*. Boston, MA: Harvard Business School Press.

Ulrich, D., Zenger, J., & Smallwood, N. (1999). *Results-based leadership*. Boston, MA: Harvard Business School Press.

Zingheim, P. K., & Schuster, J. R. (2000). *Pay people right: Breakthrough reward strategies to create great companies*. San Francisco, CA: Jossey-Bass.

Notes:

Notes:

Notes:

In addition to

FYI for Performance Management™

Lominger International: A Korn/Ferry Company offers these products:

- **PERFORMANCE MANAGEMENT ARCHITECT® Sort Cards**, to facilitate training or group processes. The *PMA Quick Reference Guide* provides guidelines for using the PMA Sort Cards.

- **The PMA Placemat Set:** The three placemats illustrate the application of the 10 Universal Performance Dimensions in the primary performance management phases—planning and goal setting, feedback and coaching, and performance review.

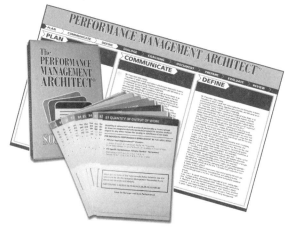

- *FYI for Your Improvement™* 4th **Edition Book**
- *Broadband Talent Management: Paths to Improvement* **Book**
- *The Leadership Machine* 3rd **Edition Book**

To order, visit our Web site at:

www.lominger.com